AF504547

THE RECIPIENT OF A DONOR'S HEART

The Recipient of a Donor's Heart
Debra Lesia Judkins

Copyright © 2025 by Debra Lesia Judkins

All rights reserved.
No part of this book may be reproduced in any form or by any electronic or mechanical means, including information storage and retrieval systems, without written permission from the author, except for the use of brief quotations in a book review.

ISBN 979-8-89691-822-6

THE RECIPIENT OF A DONOR'S HEART

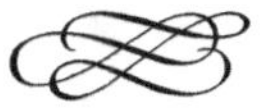

DEBRA LESIA JUDKINS

CONTENTS

DEDICATION

I dedicate this book to my husband, Larry Judkins SR. His genuine love and constant support have been my greatest source of strength and inspiration.". He has brought so much fun into my plans and projects and has always taken the time to care for what really matters.

I feel incredibly lucky when I think about all he has done and how much he has meant to me since the day he came into my life. He has shown the significance of our marriage and his commitment to engaging in actions that contribute to our mutual growth.

Larry, a husband, set aside for me to find, and yet he found me. Over the years, we have had many talks. He has always reminded me of my various talents and encouraged me to enjoy and make the most of whatever I was working on. Whenever I experienced boredom, he helped me transition to my next endeavor. The choices I made throughout my life are a testament to the wife I am to him today. He is an exceptional husband, encouraging me not to be afraid and reassuring me that no challenge is too great for me to manage. He has motivated me to exceed my dreams, even at the mature age of sixty-seven. During our forty-four years together, he continues to discover and help develop my talents.

ABOUT THE AUTHOR

Debra McGrone-Judkins, known to many as "Inndiah," began her writing journey in the mid-1970s. Her mother was the first to notice her daughter's numerous talents, and it was through this recognition that Debra's passion for writing blossomed. Despite her natural skill for storytelling, Debra often wrote her pieces only to set them aside and begin anew with the next story.

In addition to her literary pursuits, Debra also delved into the world of music. She started a singing career that showcased her talents on a broader scale and took her to new heights. Her artistic expression was not confined to writing and singing; she also embraced acting, performing in various plays and writing numerous play manuscripts.

Debra's diverse talents have taken her across the globe, enriching her experiences and broadening her perspectives. "This is her first published novel," a testament to her dedication and love for story-telling. Her journey is a captivating narrative of creativity, resilience, and boundless talent, making her a multifaceted artist whose work continues to inspire.

POEM

REACHING FOR WHAT IS ACHIEVABLE

When you reach for what is achievable, nothing is certain. Yet, when the reachable becomes the achieved, you have conquered battles and triumphed in the war.
Close your eyes. Extend your arms. Flap them as if they were wings, wings that dare to defy gravity. Fly high among the birds of prey.
Let your imagination travel, unbound and free, as if you were a bird soaring unseen over untouched lands and untold worlds, where no man's eyes have wandered.
For those who have wings, do not give in. Do not falter. You can rise beyond because when the reachable becomes achievable, doubt no longer lingers. It fades away, and victory reigns.
Your imagination is the bridge to reality, a flight that begins with faith and vision.

By Debra Lesia Judkins

PREFACE

This book is about two children growing up on the same street, playing in the park with all the other children. They would always find themselves playing together every time they went to the park, not realizing that they were neighbors on the same block. Whenever Passion came to the park, Gabriel was already there, waiting and watching to see if she would come. He always made sure to have a swing waiting for her. Both parents were there, watching the children as they played.

As school started, they found themselves in the same class throughout the first to fifth grade. They had this connection in junior high school and high school, continuing to be best friends. However, their parents were quite wary of this relationship. Gabriel came from a Muslim background, while Passion came from a Catholic background. They knew their parents would never agree to any kind of relationship between the two of them, so they kept it quiet as they headed off to college.

One day, both sets of parents caught them holding hands. They had wanted to surprise the kids. Passion's mom and dad were waving their hands at her, and they noticed Gabriel looking in the other direction.

They were confused about what he was looking at, and then they saw his mom and dad watching him. Gabriel knew that this one barrier—religion—could never be overcome. They could not fall in love with each other; it was forbidden. But it didn't stop them; they kept it a secret.

After their second year of college, these episodes continued. The parents could see that no matter what they said or their beliefs were, the two would always be together. So, both sets of parents allowed them to love openly and freely.

As time went on, Gabriel and Passion finished college, got married, and had two kids of their own. Those children grew up and had their own families.

Moving forward, as they became empty nesters, they started traveling and seeing some of the places they always wanted to visit. They constantly visited their children and grandchildren. However, over the years, traveling back and forth on the airplane got to be a little too much for Gabriel.

Throughout their lives, Gabriel and Passion faced numerous challenges, but the hardest one was when Passion became sick. Gabriel had to rush her to the hospital, and she became terminally ill. The neighbors on the street became concerned about what was happening to Passion when she was diagnosed with cancer.

By this time, everyone did their best to help Gabriel and Passion as she returned home. Later on, the ambulance came one night and picked up Passion to take her back to the hospital, but she didn't make it this time. Gabriel's world spiraled upside down to the point where he became bitter and hard, enclosed in his home, not understanding what had happened to his world. He started saying harsh words to his neighbors, seeing they still had their wives, holding hands and doing the things every couple does. He became bitter and said many unkind words to everyone, even though they continued to bring things to his home to help him out and periodically bring food. Paul and Jenny were Passion and Gabriel's next-door neighbors, and no matter how he treated her, Jenny still brought soup over to him to eat or whatever they had cooked for dinner that evening.

A year passed, and Jenny became sick. One day, Gabriel was looking out the window and saw an ambulance at his neighbor's house—it was Jenny. She had suffered a stroke. When she arrived at the hospital, the doctors informed her family that she wasn't going to make it. Since she was an organ donor, they kept her on life support to see where her organs could be donated.

The very next day, Gabriel, still grieving the loss of Passion, had a massive heart attack and ended up in the hospital himself. The doctors told him and his children that he needed a new heart. The doctor informed his children that they had a heart available for him if he was willing to accept it. The children signed the paperwork to accept the donor's heart. Gabriel underwent the heart transplant and began to heal, still unsure of what had happened to him.

Some time passed, and Gabriel began to feel different. He once had a feeling of hate and resentment in his heart, but now he felt love and compassion. Later in the story, Gabriel discovers that his neighbor Jenny was his organ donor—they gave him Jenny's heart. This revelation changed Gabriel's whole outlook, and he began to think back on how he had treated Jenny and his neighbors harshly. All his neighbors wanted to do was offer comforting words to him.

As Gabriel reflected on his journey, he became "The Recipient of a Donor's Heart," and with this heart, he was able to love again, healing from the broken heart that he once had.

This book has a lot of twists and turns, filled with pain, loss, and triumph. Especially when Passion returns to him in a dream to bring comfort. They had closure with a dance to their favorite song they used to dance to.

HOW WE MET

The golden light of the summer sun shined across the sky, casting long shadows over the playground. It was a day my family and I would have a picnic near the community playground. The squeaking of the swings blended with the sound of children's laughter, but my attention was on a boy standing near the swing set, Gabriel. His dark eyes locked with mine for a moment before he looked away. I was uncertain whether to speak to him or simply keep watching.

He looked around my age, maybe a little taller, with a quiet sort of confidence. I knew Mom preferred I play with the girls, but something about him made me forget that rule. Before I talked myself out of it, I jumped off the swing and walked over to where he was standing.

"Hi, my name is Passion." I stuck my hand out. My heart was beating a little fast.

Gabriel hesitated before shaking my hand, but when he did, his fingers were warm against mine. Then, with his eyes wide open, he spoke loudly, saying, "You're really pretty."

I blinked, and I was surprised. No boy had ever told me that before. A smile stretched across my face. "Thank you," I said, rocking back on my heels.

"Wanna swing? Gabriel asked, "I can push you," he offered, gazing deep into my eyes.

"Sure!"

I climbed onto the swing, and he pushed me slowly at first, then higher. We laughed, and the world around us seemed to disappear. When the other kids approached us, excited for their turn to swing, Gabriel stood firm. "No, this swing is for Passion," he declared, much to their disappointment. "Maybe later."

After what felt like forever, having fun with Gabriel, I faintly heard my mother calling me. I hopped off the swing. "I have to go. "My mom's calling," I said, glancing toward the picnic tables where my family was sitting.

"Me too," Gabriel replied, pointing to where his mother sat, watching. "Will you come back tomorrow?"

I nodded, a smile tugging at my lips. "I live nearby."

"Then I will see you again," he said, waving before running off.

After eating, I asked my mom if I could return to the swing set. She said I could but told me to be careful not to get my dress messed up because we had somewhere to go that evening. I assured her, "Okay, Mom, I will not."

We played some more, and Gabriel pushed me a little too high because when I tried to get off the swing, I fell and got my dress dirty. He looked at me and said, "Passion, I am so sorry. I did not mean to do that." I replied, "It's okay. My mom can wash it." Gabriel said, "Are you sure?" "Yes." He asked if I would be coming back again to play at the park. I said yes. He asked if I lived in the neighborhood, and I told him I did. "Then I will see you again," he said. We got back into our car and began to travel back home.

I was sitting on the steps of my house when I saw from a distance the little boy I had been playing with at the park. He waved, and I waved back, feeling a spark of excitement. "Mom, that is the little boy who played with me at the park," I said. She looked over and said, "Oh, the one who got your dress dirty and then apologized? That was sweet of him."

I asked my mom if I could ride my bike, and she said yes. Gabriel, who lived across the street, saw me getting my bike out and got his, too. We rode on our sides of the street, racing to see who could reach the corner the fastest. We laughed and enjoyed our little competition until my mom called out, "It's time to get ready for supper." I told Gabriel, "I have to go inside now and have supper. I will talk to you later." He replied, "Okay, Passion. I will see you later."

After I cleaned up and had dinner, my mom told me it was time for bed. I could not help but think about what a beautiful day it had been —a day I did not want to forget. People might think little kids do not know what love is, but I greatly liked Gabriel.

When Christmas came around, we put up a nice tree, and I noticed Gabriel did not have a Christmas tree in his window. I asked my mom why. She explained, "Passion, they have a different religion. We are catholic, and they are Muslim. They do not celebrate Christmas." "But why, Mom?" I asked. She said, "One day, when you get older, you will understand."

Determined to share the joy of giving, I always found a way to sneak a small gift for Gabriel at school. I wanted him to experience what it was like to receive a present. He never told his parents about the gift.

We went shopping for clothes and school supplies. On the first day of school, my mom packed my lunch, and I got on the bus. To my delight, Gabriel got on the bus, too. He walked past me, grinning from ear to ear, and I was grinning just as widely. I was so happy he was on the bus with me, going to the same school.

When we arrived at school, we made our way in. Gabriel complimented my book bag, and I told him I liked his too. I knew he wanted to hold my hand, and I wanted to hold his, but we had to follow the school rules.

As we went into our classroom, I realized Gabriel and I were in the same class. I was so happy because I knew then that I had a good friend.

We took our bags and put them on the shelf, which was meant for our books and school supplies. I sat down at my desk, and the teacher greeted us, "Good morning, children. Let me introduce myself. My name is Ms. Butler. I am so happy to have you all in my class. Now that we have that out of the way. I will walk down each aisle, and each of you will tell me your names." When it became my turn, I said my name was Passion. Then, the boy sitting right behind me said, "My name is Gabriel." I felt shy and did not look around like everyone else did.

Our first subject was English. The teacher asked us to pull out our books. As we read, she could tell which students needed more help. Gabriel was a little slower than me, so we helped each other out. Our teacher taught us that we should always help one another and that no one was better than anyone else. I liked our teacher; she was nice to us.

As we moved on to the next subject, I became Gabriel's helper in the classroom. Gabriel did not want anyone else to get too close to me because he said I was his friend.

Lunchtime arrived, and the lunch bell rang. We went to the lunch hall, and I opened my lunch bag to find a sandwich, a bag of chips, an apple, and two cookies that my mom had made for me. Gabriel had different food prepared by his mom. He asked if he could have half of my peanut butter and jelly sandwich. I gave it to him, and he said,

"You know, Passion, this tastes good. I've never had this before." I replied, "You haven't?" He said, "No, we do not eat food like this." I told him, "We always eat like this." Gabriel asked, "Do you think you can bring an extra sandwich for me tomorrow?"

The next day, I asked my mom to make an extra sandwich for Gabriel. She said, "That would be so nice.

After lunch, we went back to class. The teacher asked if we enjoyed our lunchtime, and we all said yes. Our next subject was math, one of my strong subjects. I knew Gabriel might have some difficulty, so I asked the teacher if I could sit next to him to show him how to use beads for counting. She said, "Yes, Passion, you can help him."

As time went on, we graduated from elementary school and moved on to junior high, but Gabriel remained my friend. Gabriel met me at the corner of my house, his hands stuffed in his pockets. His usual easy smile was missing.

"What's wrong?" I asked.

He sighed, glancing at the ground. "My mother... she told me I can't keep seeing you. She says I'm getting too close."

My stomach tightened. "Too close? What does that even mean?"

He hesitated before looking at me. "It's not... our way, Passion. My family doesn't believe in dating before marriage. And even then—" He swallowed hard. "They've already chosen someone for me."

The words hit me like a punch to the chest. "Chosen?" My voice cracked. "Like... an arranged marriage?"

He nodded, his jaw tightening.

I felt my breath hitch, and suddenly, the world blurred. I blinked fast, trying to keep the tears from falling. But Gabriel saw.

He reached out gently, his fingers tilting my chin up so I had to meet his gaze. His dark eyes were soft but filled with something deeper, something desperate.

"Passion, don't cry," he whispered. "I love you. I don't care what they say. We'll find a way."

"How?" My voice was barely audible. "They'll never accept me."

"Then I'll fight for you." He held my face between his hands. "Even if it means keeping this between us for now, I won't lose you."

I reassured him of my love for him and told him about our culture as Catholics—how two people fall in love freely but must remain pure before marriage. This is necessary in most religions.

We have stood by each other's side, from little kids to teenagers. Gabriel, we grew to what is natural, but we realized that while we were different by religion, we were also the same in many ways. I did not know what to say, so I just went along with it. Gabriel said they're Muslim, and they do not believe the same things we do.

Time went on, and we made it to high school. One day, I asked my mom, "How old were you when you met Daddy?" She replied, "Oh, Passion, I was young, just like you are today. We first met when we were young, like you and Gabriel." I said, "So, is it OK for me to have a relationship with Gabriel?" She explained, "Passion, Gabriel comes from a different religion with different traditions than we do as Catholics. They have arranged marriages; parents choose who their children will marry."

"That is not fair, Mom," I said.

She sighed, "I know, baby, but as you grow and mature, you will understand and respect their traditions as they do ours."

"But, Mama, I cannot help how my heart feels. My heart tells me he's the one for me. Who said that two hearts that love each other so much cannot be together?"

She replied, "OK, Passion, we will just wait and see."

Finally, we moved on to college. I focused on psychology while Gabriel studied computer science. One day, he came up behind me and said, "Hi Passion!" It felt like my entire world lit up just hearing him call my name. The same little boy from many years ago still called my name the same way; it meant so much to me.

We had lunch together, talking about our lives again. Gabriel reminded me that his love for me never changed. He grabbed my hands and took them to his heart. He whispered gently and softly, "Passion, you are my choice; you are the wife for me. Most of all, I love you."

I saw my parents' car pulling up to bring the book I left on the kitchen counter. I turned around to look at the time. Gabriel's eyes were fixed on something, and I realized he was looking at his parents. They looked upset. Gabriel's parents started talking and gesturing as if he had done something wrong. All he did was take my hand. He went to his parents' car, and when he came back, he looked sad. I asked, "Gabriel, what's the matter?" He said he did not want to talk about it.

My father's gaze was intense. He stated, "Your mother and I have provided you with everything. And this is how you repay us? With this lack of respect. Abandoning your duty as a Muslim? What about the shame you bring to our family?" Silence stretched between them. Passion wanted to reach for Gabriel's hand, but she didn't. Not yet.

His mother spoke softly, "If you love her, prove it. Not with words. With time."

"Why, Dad? By following my own heart?" My voice was steady, but I felt unsettled inside.

"Gabriel, we have chosen a wife for you, and she has accepted you for her husband. You will marry her."

"That is where you are wrong. I am a US citizen, given my own rights. I will not let you draw a line for me to follow behind you."

Later that night, I did not know why he was upset, so I told my mom about it. She asked, "Passion, I told you they're from a different culture. They do not believe in relationships before marriage. Whatever feelings you have for him aren't going to go anywhere." I replied, "Mom, whatever it is, I am going to break through that. I really believe we can be a couple."

Gabriel sat down with me at a garden table the next day at college. He explained to me about the big argument he had with his parents. He explained to me, "They threatened to send me away if they saw me with you again. They opposed our relationship from the start. I stood up to my father and told him, "You cannot control my heart. You did not put it there."

"There is something else I need to tell you. They have chosen a wife for me to marry. I became confused and shaken by the words coming out of my parents' mouths. I looked at my mother, her head bowed down, and she said, "It's time for you to go."

Tears ran down my face. I agreed to meet the woman they wanted me to marry—the one my parents promised me to. They were confused because I had fallen deeply in love with a woman forbidden by my religious upbringing. But the girl, too, was not ready and confused to accept the proposal because, in my culture, we dared not turn it down, as it would bring shame upon the family.

I beg my mom and dad. "Please. If you love me as you have shown me. Then please, love me enough to allow me to choose." My father and mother went into another room. At first, I thought they were disgusted with me. I just sat on the floor praying, praying that something good would come from this. Finally, after two hours, my parents came out, and my dad said, "Gabriel," "Yes, Dad." "You are in love with this girl?" "Yes, Dad." My mom asked the same question. I gave her the same answer. Suddenly, my dad said they would like me to meet with Passion's parents. I could not believe what I was hearing. I began to cry. My heart opened to hopes and dreams. Happy with my parents' decision. Now I see why my parents would drive to school every day around lunchtime to see what I was doing. Each time, they found us together, and this went on for several months and a year.

One day, Gabriel came to me with some good news. "My mom and dad sat down with me," he said. "They told me they've been watching us since we were little kids, seeing how we always played together and cared for each other. They did not think much about it. Because we were just kids, they realized that, despite our differences, we had grown close. They decided to allow me to love openly and freely as long as I continue my studies and not let them get in the way." I told him, "I will not let my studies get in the way." And they still wanted to meet your parents formally.

A week goes by. Finally, both sides of the family meet at a beautiful restaurant. Everyone is just looking at one another. Passion's father came up to my father to shake his hand. My Mom graced Passion's mom with a hug.

"So, Princess, what I am trying to tell you is that, despite my past experiences and the initial resistance, my mom and dad have finally decided to allow me to love you openly and freely. I believe there is a big chance for us."

"Oh God, I am so happy!" It just made my day. There is so much joy in my heart. My spirits have improved immensely because it feels like a burden has been lifted off me. I know I have found my true love, and I am able to love him openly, accepted by his family, just as my family has accepted him.

Both of our families have embraced our relationship. We all grew up around each other in the neighborhood, never realizing that children can bring so much happiness into our lives. Growing together, we've learned to love beyond all barriers and boundaries. I now know that distance and obstacles do not matter when you genuinely love someone. True love can break through all walls and find its way to the hearts it belongs to.

"I am forever grateful for my parent's decision to allow me to love you because I truly believe that nothing can break that bond when two hearts are connected. You know, Passion, you are going to be the one I love for the rest of my life now that my parents have accepted you and our love."

"Three weeks have passed, Passion, and my mother and father would like to sit down with your mother and father to talk about the both of us. I am almost certain that everything will go well, and I hope so because we have their blessing to be in love and, hopefully, in marriage as well."

We finally made it over to your house and were greeted warmly. Neither side knew who would speak first or what anyone would say, but the conversation got started. I saw your mother look at you as if she was saying, "My son is in love." I turned and looked at your father as if he was saying, "My son has chosen who he wants to love for himself." To go against tradition, he found himself making decisions for himself. Times have changed, and people are falling in love with who they want to love without being told who to love.

Your mother said to me, "Do you love my son?" and your father asked the same thing. I said, "With all my heart." The look on both their faces assured me that it was OK to love you. My parents looked at each other and then at your parents with amazing looks on their faces. There was a man and woman with a handsome son, willing to allow their son to love our daughter despite all the stigma surrounding their traditional way of life. Knowing that we had broken this barrier was such a great feeling. Little did I know that while they were talking to me, I was asking God to put it upon them to let them love me.

They led us into the dining area, where someone had prepared a big meal for us. I did not realize that a dinner table could be so pretty and colorful. In some way, I guess they already knew it was a done deal by allowing us to become one.

We finally finished dinner and went back into the living room. They made this nice hot tea; some called it chai. It had such a beautiful aroma and a taste that was out of this world. It was time for us to get ready to go home.

"Gabriel, thank you for this beautiful evening. I know where the second chapter of my life will be heading—we will become one, joined together in marriage."

The night air was crisp, carrying the scent of jasmine as we stood beneath the soft glow of the garden lights. Gabriel fidgeted, his hands trembling slightly.

"What's wrong?" I asked, half-laughing. "You look nervous."

He exhaled, then took my hands in his. "Passion, do you know how long I've loved you?" His thumb brushed over my palm. "Since the day you made me chase you around that swing set."

A small laugh escaped me, but my heart pounded as he slowly sank to one knee.

"Gabriel…"

"I don't have a perfect speech," he admitted, his voice husky and emotional. "All I know is that my life makes sense when I'm with you. We've made it through every memory, fight, and stolen moment. And I don't want to do life without you." He pulled out a small velvet box and opened it, revealing a delicate diamond ring that caught the moonlight. "Will you marry me?"

Tears burned my eyes. "Yes, Gabriel. A thousand times, yes."

"Yes, I will, Gabriel."

"Passion, let us plan our wedding in June. Let us make it colorful to show the world all the colors that surround our love—all the flowers that bloom, the dandelions that cover the ground, the tulips that grow, and the rose bushes that continue to blossom. Let their beauty speak for us, as our love is like that multitude of flowers that continue to blossom."

"OK, Gabriel, it's so beautiful."

"I know that the colors you choose for our wedding will be beautiful because you have impeccable taste and style. I've watched you through the years and how you dress very respectfully, never too revealing, always with good taste. You know, Passion, when you speak, I love to hear the tone of your voice because you speak with so much integrity, the kind of voice that you can listen to today in and day out."

"Stop, Gabriel. You are going to make me start crying."

"That is all right, Passion. When I look at you and see that beauty, it could make any man cry. You are the flower I chose, one I know I will water for the rest of my life. Another flower will try to blossom for every teardrop that falls and hits the ground. I promise you, Passion, that no matter what storms we may go through in our lives, we will find the strength to make it through. After the storm passes and we see what is left, we will gather it up and stand tall because our love will find its way."

Our wedding day has finally come—all the colors we picked out. My mom and future mother-in-law are working together. To make sure my wedding gown is perfectly laid out, the bridesmaids' dresses are fitted beautifully, and Dad and my future father-in-law are with the grooms-men. I know, this is going to be the wedding of all weddings. I cannot wait to have my dad walk me down the aisle. And for Gabriel to see me in my wedding dress. He is going to be shocked, and I know it's going to bring him to tears. I hear the music playing—a song that has resonated with us since our younger years, a song only we understand due to the journey it took us to get to where we are. I do not want to start getting emotional right now. I just want to get there and see him at the altar. My dad walked me into my wedding hall. I saw Gabriel at the altar. As I began walking closer, we both did our best. To hold back tears. I finally made it to him. When the time came for us to say our vows. We began to say our vows to one another. It was Gabriel's turn to go first. They read as follows: I look into your face, fighting back every tear. "What's wrong, Gabriel? Why are you crying? Are those happy tears? What's going on?"

"Passion, I wrote the vows I wanted to tell you but cannot. I cannot take my eyes off you to read these vows. Let me just speak it from my heart. You are so beautiful, a bride I chose for myself. I just cannot hold back the tears." My parents stood up and spoke. "She is loved, my son; you have chosen." The beauty I see standing before me feels surreal. Could God have created such a beautiful person, a beautiful woman, just for me? It's got to be real. "Passion our love is like a story-book, waiting to be written.

"Are you going to be okay?"

I replied, "Yes. You see, all my life, from childhood, I've loved this woman. We've had the blessing from both sides of our family to love openly, and today, I want the world to know that I have chosen this woman to love. One that is going to last a lifetime. At this time, Gabriel and I cannot stop crying.

"Okay, Gabriel, can we continue with the ceremony?" I asked. yes

Its Passions turn, lowering the piece of paper she had in her hands. She begins to speak her vows from her heart, looking him in the eyes. Her words began to tear open a deeper dimension in Gabriels's heart. Even the guest began to cry. Passion continues. "Gabriel, from the little girl that became your playmate, your best friend. Who knew this day was even possible? We've broken down walls and torn open barriers. We went on against tradition, with the support of our parents giving us their blessing." I look to them and thank them for their support. "Gabriel, when your heart beats, my heart follows the same rhythm. When you breathe, love tells me. Both of our chests rise and come down at the same time. I stood back, waiting and hoping that God would make a way for us to be joined together. You will be joyful when I wake up in the morning, my peace throughout the day and my happiness when I fall asleep at night. When I am sleeping, I only want to think that you are mine, my husband, the man I chose for myself. Happiness is when that woman finds a loyal friend—a lover of the heart. Our love is like playing with a deck of cards. Initially, you only look for the two hearts and a diamond."

"Okay, now that we're done with the vows, can we get the rings?" Gabriel asked.

Gabriel placed the ring on my finger, and I put his ring on his finger. With that, we said to each other, "We are now one—one light, one understanding, one peace."

Heading to the reception hall, the photographer is waiting so we can photograph the wedding party. Everything is so beautiful. He finally finished taking all the pictures, and we entered this beautiful room that was decorated especially for us. Spot-on words cannot describe it. I look up; flowers are just hanging from the ceiling, and the beautiful gold in this room is enough to light up anyone's life.

"Look at my cake, Gabriel. It's so beautiful! I've never seen such a big cake. As you know, Passion, we have two hundred guests, and we must have enough to accommodate everyone, but it's so huge! Gabriel, you like it?"

"I love it, Gabriel."

We begin to walk over to the cake. Gabriel slices the first piece and puts it into my mouth, and I put a piece into his. Lights were flashing all around us, and people were taking pictures. I can hardly believe something so beautiful. We make it to our table and sit down; it's like we are Prince and Princesses. Listen to all the laughter around us, everyone joining in our celebration, a special day set aside for us.

"Gabriel, have you noticed the clock over there? Isn't that when we started to walk into our wedding?"

"Yes, Passion, it is. It's still standing there. And no, Passion, it will not start back up again until our day is finished, as this time is set aside for us."

It's time now to bring our wedding party to a close, but before we can do that, we have some gifts to open, not all of them, but some. Gabriel hands me one of the gifts and says,

"Passion, you open it."

To my surprise, it was a gift from my mother and father-in-law: a golden necklace with earrings. So beautiful. Tears begin to fall down my face, and Gabriel says,

"Passion, do not mess up your makeup, do not cry. It's going to be okay. It is my mother and father expressing their gratitude and happiness that they have a new daughter in the family." I do not know what to say. It's something I've never seen before. "Gabriel, can we open the rest of our gifts at home?"

"Sure, Passion. I am ready to go."

THE BEGINNING OF A NEW CHAPTER

We make it to the front door of the reception hall. Waiting for us is a limousine to take us home. As we ride back to the house, we realize that the limousine is just taking us to his mom and dad's home. We turn down a street with all these beautiful homes, and it pulls up. In view, I see my mother-in-law and father-in-law standing in the doorway. We try to figure out what's going on.

"Why did the limousine bring us here?"

"Come on in," she says to both of us.

As we enter the front door, we are amazed at the home; it is so beautiful. The furniture, everything, is unbelievable.

"Come on, I want to show you something," my mother-in-law says.

She knows that every woman loves a beautiful kitchen, so she brings me into her kitchen and says,

"You like the new kitchen?"

"Yes, Mom, it is beautiful."

"I thought you would like that."

Both she and my father-in-law say,

"Passion, Gabriel, this is our gift to you. This is your new home. This is where you will start the second chapter of your life. It will be the home where you raise your children. We just want you to be happy. Please accept our generosity."

I could not believe what I was hearing. I started crying constantly. Never in my wildest dreams did I expect anything like this. It feels like I am living in a dream, hoping I'll never wake up, but to my eyes, it is real. My new mother-in-law and father-in-law then say,

"It is time for us to leave, so you can spend this time alone."

Gabriel and I walk throughout the whole house, still shaking our heads in disbelief that we have a home to call ours.

"Gabriel, we need to pack our things, but we left everything at your parents' home."

He said, "No, our suitcases are here. They brought them to us because they knew we were heading out in the morning. We do not have anything to worry about."

"Where are we going?" I asked.

He said, "I am not sure. There is a package on the kitchen counter that Mom and Dad left for us."

We opened it up and found a beautiful honeymoon package for traveling to the Seven Seas.

"You know I love being on the water. I love being on a boat, but I never thought I would ever have the opportunity to be on a big ship traveling the Seven Seas. But now, I do believe that some dreams do come true."

"Passion, I just love looking at you. The excitement on your face is like that of a little girl who's been given her first doll. Every gift you receive is like something you have never seen or had before, and that is the excitement I love to see on your face. No matter what I give you, small or big, you accept it without judgment."

"Well, I am tired. Let us just relax a little bit and enjoy being in our house."

"Okay, Gabriel. Oh, by the way, did you see our jacuzzi? We have a special area in the house with a jacuzzi just for us."

"Really? Let us go check it out."

We go to the jacuzzi, which is big enough for ten people but is all ours.

"Passion, would you like to get into it?"

"Oh yes, Gabriel, I would love that."

We got undressed, put on a few clothes, and slid into the jacuzzi, just enjoying the moment. It was such a warm feeling. We could not stay in too long for fear we might doze off, and that is not a good thing. We got out of the jacuzzi and dried off. It is time to go to bed.

Gabriel said, "Would you like to take a nice warm shower to loosen up a little bit? You know, get all the makeup and everything off."

"Sure, Gabriel."

He bathed my body, using every finger as if they were magnets, finding every tense spot and relieving the tightening muscle. This is all new to me because I have never had a man bathe me. It was like he was hitting every spot on my body, and my body began to tremble.

"What's happening to me?"

Finally, we finished the shower. I put on a beautiful gown and my favorite sweet perfume, which he loves so much. We got in bed, and Gabriel reached over, grabbed me, and held on to me so tightly. I did not know what to expect at that moment, but he just held me. We were not planning to do anything until we were ready. We just talked to each other throughout the night until we fell asleep.

Time goes by, and we finally make it to our honeymoon destination. What a beautiful place. As we exited the plane, the attendants rolled out this beautiful red carpet. I thought for a moment that there was some royalty on our flight, only to realize it was for us.

"Passion, yes. My parents set all this up for us. They wanted us to experience what life was like in Malaysia. My mother grew up here. I know we will have the time of our lives, taking as many pictures as possible."

The chauffeur took us to the villa where we would be staying, complete with our own private cook. We had such a good time, experiencing so much—though not everything—but enough to sustain us until we could come back and see the rest.

It is time to head back home. I looked at Gabriel and said, "I am blessed, truly blessed, to have so much when so many people have so little. I am blessed because of the endless love and the bond we've had since childhood. Who has that? Not many people. I know that our journey through this life will be good."

Gabriel and I talked about having a family. He asked me how many children I would love to have, and I asked Gabriel, "How many children would you like to have?" He replied, "As many kids as your body can deliver."

I said, "What do you mean by that?"

"I am just kidding. I would like to have a son and a daughter."

"OK, that sounds reasonable."

We began the next chapter of our life. We planned to have our first baby. Months passed, and I became pregnant with our first child, a son. We named him Jabril. He was born one year before the day of our wedding anniversary, a beautiful and handsome son. We brought him home from the hospital, full of joy, just watching to see what we created. As Jabril grew, he started crawling and getting into things like little boys do. It was a joy to see him crawling around. He wasn't much of a crybaby; he was a happy baby. Gabriel would come home from work, and Jabril just knew that Daddy was coming through the door. He heard the doorbell and the keys jingling, and he would start crawling, knowing Daddy was coming through that door. He would lie on the floor because he knew it was Daddy. Gabriel would pick him up and hold him tight. Jabril said "Dada" for the first time because he always said "Mama."

Jabril will turn two years old in a couple of months, and I want to plan his first birthday party with little kids and family to come over and celebrate this special day. Not that he will remember it, but it is something to have in our collection of memories. For some reason, I am feeling tired today. I do not know what's going on with me. It is like I do not have a lot of energy. I am not sure if I am coming down with something or if it is the flu. I hope not because I do not want the baby to get sick. This has lasted for a few days and is not improving. I told Gabriel that I needed to see a doctor and that there was something they could give me to help. So, I made an appointment to see my doctor. Two days later, I went in, and the doctors ran many tests. They drew blood and sent it to the lab. The doctor said she would let me know by the end of the day or before the end of the day what was going on to see if I had an infection in my body.

When I got home, the phone rang before I could walk through the door. Gabriel answered the phone and said, "Passion, it is the doctor's office calling about your test results."

"Oh, OK, hold on for a second. Let me take the call."

I took off my coat and proceeded to take the phone.

"Yes, this is Passion."

"We got your test results. Congratulations! You do not have the flu or anything, but you are expecting. You are pregnant."

I looked at Gabriel, and he looked at me. He said, "What's going on? What's the matter?"

"I do not have the flu. I am not sick; I am pregnant."

He looked at me and laughed. "You are kidding. No, you are not."

"Yes, I am pregnant."

"Oh, my goodness, we are having both of our babies so close together."

"Yes, but it is good because at least they can grow together."

The rest of the day was filled with excitement about having another baby. We were so happy and overjoyed that we shared the good news with our parents. You would think they were having a baby, too.

Nine months passed. We did not want to know what we were having this time; we just wanted it to be a surprise, whatever God blessed us with. We were so happy, and as you know, a baby girl was born. We named her Saida, a beautiful name. We brought her home, and both our parents were at home watching over Jabril. We opened the door, and little Jabril was there waiting to greet his little sister. He kept yelling, "Baby, Mama!"

I said, "Yes, baby. Get on the couch so you can hold your baby sister."

We placed Jabril on the couch, set him up in the corner so he had support on each side, and placed Saida in his arms. He kissed her on the forehead and said, "Saida." It was so beautiful to hear him say his sister's name.

"OK, Jabril, we have to take the baby because she has to be fed, and she is hungry."

"No, Mommy, no. Saida, stay with me."

"Would you like to feed her?"

"Yes, Mommy."

We gave him her bottle, and he gently held it in her mouth. I could not help myself; I had to take a picture of him holding his sister. I knew he was going to be a protector of her. He will look back on this picture and say, "Mom, this was one of the happiest days I had been a big brother. Holding my little sister." Jabril was getting tired, so I grabbed Saida and placed her in her bassinet, and Gabriel put Jabril down for a nap. Family members and friends started coming over to greet the new baby and celebrate.

"You did not need to bring gifts. We have so many already. Thank you. Come on in and take a seat. There are refreshments in the kitchen if you would like something to drink or eat."

"We are so happy that you and Gabriel finally have your daughter, and I know Gabriel is thrilled."

"Yes, Jenny, he is very happy."

"Paul, what is it that you have?"

"Well, Passion, it is something I made especially for Saida when she gets a little older. I know everyone is bringing things that she can use now, but I am looking a little further ahead. When she finally gets her first doll, she will have a little baby bassinet just like the one she's in that she can put her baby doll in."

"Oh, Paul, that is so thoughtful of you. But how did you know how her bassinet looked if you had never seen it?" "Jenny and I were at the same shopping center you and Gabriel were at. We watched and saw the basinet she put in your cart, so we knew exactly how to build it based on that picture. I guess people watch you, and you never know it."

"I am really touched that you both would build something so beautiful. It is identical to her own bassinet."

"You know, Passion, when our little girl was growing up, Paul stayed in the garage constantly building toys, especially for her. He wanted her to have everything and those things to be special, so he built them. He knew no one else would ever have anything like that or think of building something so personal. I built all our son Tim's toys too, most of his cars and trucks. My greatest one was the big tractor he wanted. I built one that he could drive in. He was the happiest little boy. He had something daddy built for him that no one else had."

I used to tell him all the time that she was going to be a spoiled child in the family. He would just laugh and say she was Daddy's little girl, and she'd not want for anything. She would have it all.

"Passion, you need to be sitting down and resting. You just came home from the hospital; let us do all the work."

"I just cannot sit down right now. I am enjoying you all being here celebrating with me and Gabriel."

"Come on, Passion, go into the kitchen with me. I could bring the refreshments out so everyone can relax and have a good time. That way, everyone is not crowded into the kitchen."

"OK, let me help you."

"Passion, did you do all this?"

"Come on, Jenny, you know I did not do this. Our parents set everything up for us, so when I came home, I did not have to worry about anything. I really thank them for that."

"OK, that is great. You had me worried there for a moment."

"But look at you now, Passion. You have this special glow about you. Being a parent now, you have your son, and now you have a daughter. I am so happy for both of you."

"Is that another knock at the door?"

"I believe so, Passion."

"Gabriel, can you see who's at the door?"

"Sure, Passion, no problem."

"Hi, Sarah and Tim, come on in. I did not expect to see you here. How did you hear about Passion coming home today?"

"Well, Gabriel, to be honest, your parents put this together and let everyone know she was coming home. We wanted to surprise her."

As the gathering came to an end, family and friends began to leave one after the other. Our parents cleaned the house while I rested on the couch.

"Gabriel,"

"Yes, sweetheart?"

"Can you get me a cup of coffee?"

"Sure. Would you like anything else with it?"

"Yes, I better try to eat something. I am starting to feel a bit hungry. I just did not want any snack food."

"You do not have to worry about that. Our parents have already prepared dinner for all of us. So, when we are ready to eat, we will have something balanced."

"That was so sweet of them."

"Passion,"

"Yes, Gabriel?"

"Thank you so much for giving me a son and a daughter. We are a complete family now. You know, Passion, everything we have gone through to get to where we are today, was worth it."

The kids are growing and getting bigger. I really love living on the ranch, free from city life. I know there will be a time when we will gradually decide whether we should move there. Our kids would have a better chance at many opportunities living there.

JOYFUL SOUND OF A COMPLETED FAMILY

The kids are growing and getting bigger. I really love living on the ranch, free from city life. I know there will be a time when we will gradually decide whether we should move there. Our kids would have a better chance at many opportunities living there.

The kids wanted to go and get the eggs from the chickens. Jabril and Saima asked if they could have scrambled eggs and toast for breakfast. They put on their boots, grabbed their baskets, and headed to the chicken coop. Each of them obtained four eggs, smiling from ear to ear. We brought them into the house. We prepared breakfast together and had so much fun cooking. Saima asked, "When school starts on Monday, will I be in the same class as Jabril?"

I said, "No. Each one of you will be in different grades and will have different teachers."

Their eyes got big with excitement. "I thought you both would feel bad."

"No, Mommy."

The first day came. Wearing their new backpacks and carrying lunch, they stood outside waiting for the bus to come. There were so many kids; everyone was happy to see each other. The bus arrived, and they boarded it. I waved and said, "Have a good day."

It's time to do some housework. School will be letting out at 2:30, and the bus is expected to have them home by 3:45. I made dinner early because the kids will be hungry. I heard the bus coming. I know they will have a lot to tell me about their first day of school.

Jabril and Saima came running into the house to tell me about their wonderful day at school today. "Mom, our teachers are nice."

"They are?"

"Yes, we're going to have fun this year at school. We have new friends we met during recess."

"I am so happy to hear you had an enjoyable day at school. What are your teachers' names?"

Jabril said his teacher's name was Miss Jacobs, and Saima had Miss Conway.

"Oh, by the way, Mom, we have some paperwork that you need to fill out for us."

"OK. Take it out of your backpack so I can fill it out, then put it back to avoid forgetting it in the morning."

"Are you hungry?"

"No, not right now, Mama. Can we go out and ride our bikes?"

"OK, just for a little while."

"Could we have an hour outside, please, Mama?"

"Stay on the street and within the neighborhood."

"We will."

The kids returned to the house after spending some time playing outside. I know they should have a good appetite now. I told them to take off all their dirty clothes and get their baths done. They finished all that and came down to have dinner.

"Mama, where's Daddy?"

"He should be pulling up in the driveway any time."

"OK. I cannot wait to tell him about our first day at school."

"I know he's going to be just as excited as you were."

Daddy made it inside the house just as Mama was putting everything on the table.

"Hi, Daddy."

"Hi, everybody. Jabril, Saima, how was your first day at school?"

"We had fun, Daddy. We met a lot of kids, and we have different teachers."

"Well, of course, you will have different teachers because you are in different grades. I am so happy that your first day of school went very well. You see, you two were worried about the other kids' liking you."

"Let's eat, but did we forget something?"

"Sorry, Dad. We need to say our blessings."

We finished dinner, and the kids watched a short movie on TV. Bedtime came, and they headed to their bedrooms. I went in to check on them to make sure they were covered up and kissed them goodnight.

"Gabriel,"

"Yes, sweetheart?"

"How was your day at work today?"

"It was pretty good, not bad at all."

"It makes me feel so good that everyone had a good day. What did you do today?"

"I did a little housework and went out to do a little shopping. There were a few things I needed to pick up at the grocery store. I see I'm going to need to go back to the store because the kids told me they don't want to have lunch in the cafeteria. They want to bring their lunch from home, and that's fine. I'll prefer that, so I know exactly what they're eating."

Five years have passed, and our kids are in the 6th and 7th grades. They are growing so fast. Before you know it, they will be in high school.

The kids are 15 and 16 years old now. Gabriel and I bought them the horses they had been wanting for a long time. They don't know we have them already. So, we will surprise them by taking them back to the ranch where we used to live. The new family that moved into our old home allowed us to rent the stable for the horses. Today is Sunday. When the kids come home from the store, we will tell them about the people who bought our old house. They have something to show us. Gabriel smirked, knowing it would be emotional for them, something they always wanted.

We made it there. The owners had the horses out of the stable. Jabril and Saima jumped out of the car and said, "Mom, Dad, they have horses."

"No, Jabril. Those are your horses."

"Come on, tell me you are joking, Dad."

"It is not a joke. You can ride them anytime."

"What are their names?"

"That is for you to choose."

"Dad, I already know the name."

"Ok, what might that be?"

"Stallion."

"And you, Saima?"

"I will name her Beauty."

"Those are some nice names."

We let the kids' bond with the horses for the remainder of the day. The ride back home was quiet. I could see Saima with tears running down her face. Jabril holding her hand, telling her, "We got our dream horses. I can't wait to tell my friends at school. Almost all of my friends at school have horses."

We made it back home and got our showers out of the way.

"Mom?"

"Yes?"

"I have something to ask. One of my friends at school is having a birthday party. Her name is Chelsea. She gave me an invitation to her birthday party on Saturday. Can I go to it?"

"Yes, you can go, but first, I need to meet her parents."

"You met her parents before, Mom. Her dad is the basketball coach at school, and her mom works in the office at school. Do you remember when you came to school on Tuesday to bring my lunch because I forgot it and left it on the counter?"

"Yes."

"Well, the lady you talked to in the office was Chelsea's mom. She said you had a long conversation with her. And she told you I was an A student."

"OK, baby. Yes, you can go to her birthday party. Is there anything in particular you would like to get her for her birthday party?"

"No school stuff, Mom."

"I understand. So, what would you like to get her?"

"She has been talking about a movie they're showing at the theater. If you want to go, I was thinking about getting her tickets to that movie. What do you think, Mom?"

"I think that would be nice."

"Thank you, Mom."

Saturday came, and Saima went to Chelsea's birthday party. She had a wonderful time. Chelsea really enjoyed her gift. She told Saima it was the best gift because it's what she really wanted. She asked Saima if she would like to come too. She said, "Yes, of course, if you want me to." The following Saturday, they went to the movies and had one of the best days, enjoying the movie, and after that, they went bowling. From that point forward, they developed a close and enduring friendship.

Jabril joined the basketball team. They won first place in their division. He was so happy. It really helped their team because he was the tallest kid on the team. He had a few friends that he would hang out with on the weekends. Parents would take turns driving the boys to the youth center to ensure they have activities to stay engaged. We never had to consider this issue because we were preoccupied with ensuring that their homework remained properly organized so they wouldn't be kicked off the team. They knew that was one of the main things the coach always told them.

"If you can't stay focused and keep your grades up, the reason why you come to school, then you could not play on the team. Not only basketball but any after-school sports."

"Jabril?"

"Yes, Dad?"

"You sound almost like a grown man with that deep voice."

Gabriel laughs. "Well, you know, Dad, I am growing. And so is my voice. There's something else I want to talk to you about when you get a moment."

"I have time. You can talk to me now. What is it?"

"Well, being a senior in high school, there are a lot of things going on. I wanted to ask you and Mom if it's OK if I can go to the prom."

"Is it that time already?"

"Yes, Dad."

"Is there someone you have in mind you want to take?"

"Yes, I do."

"What do you mean by that?"

"Nothing, Dad. She's just pretty, and I think she likes me."

"OK, I don't have a problem with it. I want you to enjoy your senior year. You know the junior and senior prom are together. Do you think Saima might want to come?"

"No, she will have her senior prom. That one is more memorable."

Senior prom took place, and Jabril and his date were dressed in peach and white attire. It was a notable sight to observe them together. They mention it is the colors they want to take their senior pictures in. They asked, "Why wouldn't you want to take it with your cap and gown?" Both said it at the same time. "That's outdated." So, I left it alone. It was his graduation.

Gabriel hired a chauffeur to take them and three other couples to the prom. He didn't want anyone to worry about driving.

Graduation day came, and I saw that my son had grown so much to his handsome young man. Move it on to another level of education, where he wants to pursue a career in physics. It was a wise decision for him because he always loves playing with numbers and can solve some of the most complicated formulas.

He was accepted into the college of his choice for his Master's in physics.

Another Year has passed, and Saima is preparing for her school prom and getting ready for graduation.

Saima and her friends decided to go to the prom together. All of them were dressed in beautiful colors. Gabriel provided the same chauffeur he did for Jabril's prom. After prom, the chauffeur drove the girl home. Saima asked me if she could have her graduation pictures done differently from Jabril's. I said, "Yes, of course. What do you want to change?"

"Mama, I want my pictures taken outside. We plan to wear our school class tie pin. I wanted to wear it on my gown, just like the rest of my friends."

Another day has come. Saima wakes up and runs into my room. I ask her what's wrong.

"It's today."

"What is today, Saima?"

"I'm supposed to have my Graduation pictures done today at 4:00 PM."

"OK, we'll make it. After all, you just wanted to wear your cap and gown."

"So you won't have a problem taking me?"

"No, there won't be a problem—not for my little girl."

"Thanks, Mom."

"Saima, I have to ask you something."

"What might that be, Mama?"

"You haven't said much about your college choice."

"I know I forgot, Mom. I'm sorry."

"I chose the University of Michigan. My dream is to become a chemist. Who knows, I might pursue a doctorate in this field."

"That would be wonderful; I would be so proud of you."

"With you and your brother being gone. It's going to be quiet in the house."

"You know, Mom, with me and Gabriel gone, it gives you and Dad a chance to get out and do some things and travel and not just sit around the house worrying about what we're doing. You all have given up so much, Mama. Look where we are today. We kept our heads on straight and stayed focused."

"I remember you and Dad talking about the first things we're going to do after we leave the house and go on to college. Do you remember that, Mom?

"Jabril and I talked about it all the time. You and Dad have given so much and helped people. It's time to think about yourselves. Take that trip overseas and see as much as you can. You told Jabril and me to never put off tomorrow what you can do today."

"They really do feel that it's a good idea. We might just do that. I want to visit Denmark. We'll go."

"See mom? There you have it. Go and enjoy yourself."

Years have passed. Jabril and Saima finished college. They both received doctoral degrees in their field.

They ended up getting married and having their own children, which gave us another reason to travel.

"Passion,"

"Yes, Gabriel."

"We have truly entered the stage of being empty nesters."

"Yes, we are."

"Sometimes, when I'm out in the flower garden, listening to all the young children playing in the neighborhood, I think back to when they were small. I would have the greatest smile on my face because, in my mind, I could see and hear them playing."

"Passion, we have each other, sweetheart. One thing is for sure: We're not going to stop living because they are gone. We're going to take adventures, travel, and enjoy the world while we can. We just have to choose where we want to go."

THE CLOCK THAT KEPT ME MOVING FORWARD

Sitting here with my mind going in so many different directions, I began to look around the room to try and focus on something that would ease my thoughts. I looked at the clock on the wall and began to stare at it as if it were trying to tell me something. "Tick tock, tick tock," was what I had been hearing for a while. Slowly and surely, it began to speak to me. It whispered my name, calling me out gently.

"Every time you come into this room, I become your every hour, minute, and second of every day. I have all the time you need," it said. The clock is always moving forward, never backward. So, let us begin the untold story of your life.

The morning has come, and the fresh morning dew is about to disintegrate into the air. The fresh fragrance of morning glories wafts through my windowpane. What a glorious day it is going to be. After their long night of rest, Acacia flowers greet me with their beauty. Oh, what a captivating array of colors!

It is time to head downstairs to make a cup of coffee. Gabriel said it had been done. "Come back to bed with me until it is finished," he said. I end up falling back to sleep, only to be awakened by a warm towel as he washes my face. Oh, what a warm feeling indeed! I look at the bedside table and see a cold glass of milk and a hot cup of coffee. Gabriel smiled and said, "Passion, how can two people love so deeply? Because when I wake up to you, I feel as though the doors have given us another token of strength to continue carrying on."

Passion would have this beautiful smile on her face.

"What would I do if I could not see this beauty of soul again?"

"Oh, Gabriel, do not say that. We have a lifetime to live, places to see, and journeys to travel," she said.

"Come on, let's have breakfast. Would you like to have it in your favorite place?"

"Yes, Gabriel," she replied.

This is a summons for the chef to prepare a good breakfast for us at the garden table, her favorite place.

"Gabriel, do you hear that?"

"What, Passion?"

"Someone's knocking at your heart."

"Oh, Passion, you are so romantic, and what you say to me, I just love you."

"Here comes breakfast, which the chef has prepared for us."

"Oh, my goodness, look how beautiful the strawberries are! Such a beautiful tray with my favorite bread, cheese, and butter. Just the way I like it, simple."

Finally, we had breakfast.

"Passion, let us make it back to the house to get our showers together."

"Yes, I would not have it any other way."

We stepped into the shower and began to soak each other down. We looked at each other, soaking each other down and cleansing as if we had something to say to one another, embracing this mental love-making encounter just before we were done with our showers. Gabriel grabbed my hand, leading me out of the shower, never taking his eyes off me. I looked deeply into his eyes as if they had a story to tell.

Finally, we got dressed. I hurried up and ran down the stairs to see all the birds on the fence as if they were waiting for me. I would whistle a bird song, and they would whistle back. I looked at the bedroom window and saw Gabriel watching over me. I carry on like a little child, twirling around in circles, taking in as much fresh air as I can.

Gabriel yelled out the window, "Passion!"

"Yes, Gabriel?"

"The clouds took a break today to give you all the sunshine. Give it your all. The day is young, and much needs to be done before night falls. I want to clean the flower bed and fill the bird feeders before we head into town to pick up a few things."

"Gabriel, I am ready."

"OK, Passion."

As we rode in the car, Gabriel and I began reminiscing about our younger years. Both sides of our family were against our union, but as the years went by, both sides decided to allow us to love freely and openly.

"Passion, back then, I had so much respect for your family, and I guess it was that they would send you away from me. My family was too afraid to ask if their son could date you, given religious barriers. I am so happy and blessed that we can show how much we need each other.

Gabriel's family finally realized that you would take loving care of me despite the religious barriers all those years ago yet look where we are now."

"Look, there is a parking spot. Let's Park here and enjoy walking at the market. I wonder what our children and grandkids are doing. They must be doing great."

"You know, Passion, we have some beautiful kids."

"I know, Gabriel. I really do miss them when they were young, running around the house, laughing, and playing. What fond memories and cheerful moments."

We finally gathered what we were coming for at the market and went back home.

"Gabriel, let's take a trip to see the grandkids and our children."

"Sure, Passion. I know we are not getting any younger. Hold on, Passion, there is a flower shop. You know I cannot pass by it without getting you a nice bouquet of flowers."

"Have you forgotten that you planted me a flower garden?"

"No, Passion, I have not forgotten. It is just that when I see flowers, I just want more for you. I just love the expression on your face as you smell this arrangement. Because everyone is different. Your face lights up like a little child, all excited every time."

We return to the house, where the chef has prepared a chateaubriand. This trip took longer than we thought.

"Let us wash our hands and enjoy this delicious meal."

Finally, dinner is finished.

"Now we can turn in for the night."

"Passion, yes, Gabriel, would you like to take a night shower with me?"

"How could I turn down a nice warm shower with you?"

We get into the shower, and, as always, we soak each other down and dry each other off. We put on our night clothes and forgot one important thing. We forgot to oil our bodies and massage each other, relieving each other from the tension of the day's chores. We put our clothes back on and got into bed, holding on to each other's thoughts as if we may not see each other tomorrow. As I began to close my eyes to sleep, Gabriel would say as he tucked me in his arm tightly,

"Passion,"

"Yes, Gabriel?"

"We have navigated and implied a level of maturity and conscious choices in our marriage. That wisdom is an act of loving someone so deeply. It is greater than a lifetime of knowledge. It involves deep understanding and the ability to see beyond superficial qualities."

The greatest pleasure in life is the love we have for one another. Gabriel, when you speak, I feel those words; when I hear them, they free me from any pain I may feel. When I close my eyes to sleep, I tuck you in my heart with loving thoughts. When I roll over to see that you are sleeping, I softly and gently say, "I love you."

"I know that you do, and I know that you feel it," you replied.

You mentioned maturity, saying our growth has outweighed the years we have been together. Let us say, for one second, 45 years, that speaks volumes. Who could speak on that level in our family?

"Gabriel, did you know love has a multitude of personalities with many faces? If you are not careful, people could fall into a life of deception, unaware of its destruction. I'm so glad that true love found its way into our hearts."

"It's getting late now; the morning will come soon. Let us get some sleep."

Six hours passed, and we both slept.

"Passion, I do not want to get up just yet. Your warm embrace has gotten me locked in your arms. Hold me for a while as if I am holding you too."

The morning has come, bringing fresh hope and possibilities.

"Passion, I cannot help but watch you as your eyes awaken in this warm embrace of solace."

"Let us get into the spirit of the moment," you said.

"What would that be?"

"Let us gather our things and go on an adventure to see how high a mountain we can climb at our age. It would be a challenge just to reach up as far as we can and stretch out our arms like birds of prey. Gazing at the land below from up above, everything looks so small. Nothing would be able to stop us. Just be free, free to dream with no chains or guilt."

"It's such a great feeling to have the ability to do some of those things. We have many more things to explore, and I hope God grants us enough time to see it all."

"Passion, if you really want to take this adventure, let's see a travel adviser and find out the best and safest places to travel. You know this will be a challenge. Do you think this is a bit much for us at our age?"

"No, Gabriel. We can take one step at a time until we build up the strength to climb."

"Do you think some of our neighbors would love to go on this adventure with us?"

"I'm not sure, Passion. It's something we would have to ask them."

"Ok, I will ask Jenny and Carl since they live next door. They are home a lot and take daily walks, which have built up a lot of leg strength for them. So, it would be a very good trip for both of us."

"Yes, it would be."

"Gabriel, I will head over to their house and chat with Jenny to see how she feels about it. I will call you when I'm on my way back home."

"Ok, Passion."

I knocked on the door, and Jenny answered to greet me. She said, "Hi, Passion. It's nice to see you. Come on in. Is everything ok?"

"Sure, everything is ok. I just have a question for you and Paul."

"What might that be?"

"Gabriel and I are planning an adventure. We want to do some rock climbing. I know that most people would never embark on something like this at our age, but we want to see if we can make it to one of the mountain tops."

"Oh, Passion, that would be great. What do you think, Paul?"

"It sounds like a good adventure. So, let us plan on joining you and Gabriel."

"Oh, I'm so excited. Passion, I do have to get ready to go to the DMV to renew my license. You know I have always been a donor in case something ever happens to me. Paul was a recipient of a liver transplant and has been doing great ever since. Someone had been on life support who happened to be a donor, and Paul was given his liver. So, after that, I told Paul that if anything should ever happen to me where my quality of life would cause me to live on life support, do not do that to me. Let me go and bless those who need any of my organs."

"Meanwhile, we can prepare ourselves by walking more and building ourselves up. I'm not sure about our other neighbors."

The time came; it was adventure time…

"Oh, Gabriel, this is going to be so much fun, even if we do not make it all the way."

"Oh, stop it, Passion. There you go, doubting yourself. Just think positive. Do you have everything packed up?"

"Yes, Gabriel."

Jenny and Carl are bringing out their luggage, so we might as well start loading up.

"Passion, I just love watching the expression on your face when you get so excited about the things we do. All for you, my love."

"Gabriel, it's amazing that we're taking a trip like this at our age. It just makes me feel so warm inside that we're able to do this. When you think back, a lot of people in our age group do not get opportunities like this. It's going to be fun, and I know Jenny and Carl are going to enjoy themselves as well."

"OK, come on, let's finish getting the rest of our things. Did you get all the food loaded up, too? Especially bring extra water. We never know how high we will get and realize that we ran out of water."

"Ok, we're all loaded up."

Finally, we made it to our destination, and our tour guide was there waiting for us. We sat down and talked with him. He went over a little handbook about safety and what we should and shouldn't do. Now, it's time to start our journey up the mountain. Everyone has their backpacks with all the necessities they need.

"Are you OK, Passion?"

"Yes, Gabriel. Do you have everything you need?"

"Yes, I have everything I need."

"Carl, Jenny, do you guys have everything you need?"

"Oh yes, we double-checked everything before we left the house and made sure."

"OK, let us start having fun."

Climbing the mountain, we saw different kinds of flowers and bushes —stuff we'd never seen before. It's so pretty. The smell of fresh greenery makes me wonder how many people have climbed this mountain. If they say it really is that beautiful, I think it's an understatement. It's hard to describe; it just makes you feel free.

We made it to about 3:00, about a quarter mile up, and we found this ledge where we set our bags down to relax and sip water. We just gazed at all this beautiful land. What a beautiful place! Twenty minutes have passed, and now it's time to continue our climb.

Finally, we make it as far as we want to go and set our bags down. You can tell that many people have been here because it's a flat area where people can come to relax, meditate, and just enjoy the greenery and the sense of freedom from the world below, letting their minds flow.

"Carl, Jenny, are you guys OK?"

"Oh yes, we are. We're OK, just amazed at all that we're seeing. It's so beautiful. I can say that if I never remember anything else from any trips Jenny and I have made, this tops them all."

"What about you two, Gabriel and Passion?"

"This is why we wanted to come here. We heard so many things about this place and had to see for ourselves. It's quite an understatement because it's hard to describe it in words as a land of peace."

We lay there for about an hour, looking and meditating. We spread out our picnic tablecloth and started to set our food out. It was nothing big, just a few sandwiches and water to drink. We realized we did not need any sugary drinks; we just needed water to prevent dehydration. It's hard to eat now because some people are so fascinated by what they see.

"Well, it's been three hours up here. Let us see if we can make it around to the other side of the mountain. Do you think you are all strong enough to go to the other side?"

"Well, isn't this trip about not just seeing one spot but going as far as we can around it to see each scenery from different angles? I want to be able to absorb as much as I can."

"You OK, Passion?"

"Yes, Gabriel."

"You are slowing down, and I want to make sure you are OK before we go any further."

"Oh, Gabriel, I'm going to be fine."

"Okay, Passion."

Finally, we make it to the other side of the mountain. Wouldn't you know it? We see a nest in the distance. We're not sure if it's an eagle's nest or a crow's nest, but we see their babies here and there. As the tour guide told us, whenever you see nesting, do not go close to them. So, we'll sit back and just watch. It's so beautiful and peaceful all around.

"Passion?"

"Yes, Gabriel?"

"You are breathing kind of hard. Are you OK?"

"Sure, Gabriel. I just want to sit down here for a minute and catch my breath."

"OK."

"OK, everybody, Jenny and Carl, are you guys ready to go back down?"

"Yes, we are. I think it's enough fun for the day. That is something I'm going to always treasure for the rest of my life."

"Come on, Passion, the descent will not be as bad as climbing up the mountain."

"OK, I'm just going to take my time."

"OK, make sure you do not lose footing as we descend." Passion yelled at me, "Gabriel, my foot is stuck!"

"Passion, what do you mean?"

"I stuck my foot in a little hole and cannot get it out."

"OK, hold on, I will be there."

Carl and Jenny came around to see what was going on, and I saw where Passion had gotten her foot stuck in an awkward position. As we tried to pull her foot out, she started to yell.

Carl said, "Gabriel, I think she may have sprained her ankle."

I replied, "I hope not. We do not need this right now; we're having so much fun."

The more we pulled on Passion's foot, the more we realized we had a problem. We tried to wrap something around it so the rocks and gravel around her ankle would not scratch her skin more than they already had.

At this time, Gabriel could see that Passion was under a great deal of stress, and she began to cry.

"Gabriel, is my foot broken?"

"Oh, Passion, I do not think so. At least, I hope not."

We all worked on Passion's foot for 30 minutes to free it. We finally succeeded, and Passion felt like she could walk a little bit on it, so we thought the foot was not broken. But when she went to take her second step, she fell about four feet. Luckily, she had something to grab onto and yelled, "Gabriel, I really think now that my foot is broken."

"OK, Passion. Carl, can you carry my backpack? I will try to lift Passion onto my back to get her down."

"Sure, Gabriel, not a problem."

We got down to an area where we could get some type of signal to call for help. Finally, the park ranger in the mountain area where we were was already down below, watching over everyone who was climbing the mountain. They always have some type of medic below because you never know what can happen in these mountains. They realized I was carrying Passion, so the medics and the team came up with a stretcher and retrieved Passion, bringing her all the way down. We finished our descent, and when we got down, the paramedic told us that Passion's foot looked like it was broken. Not only that but the way she was grabbing her chest, it seemed like she might have cracked a few ribs.

Gabriel felt bad because he did not really want to go on this trip, but he knew Passion wanted to go so badly. He just wanted to make her happy, as he always has. Passion turned to him, "Gabriel, I wanted to do this. This is my trip; it's not your fault; it's not Carl's or Jenny's. I just missed my footing and slipped. It doesn't mean you guys cannot continue and have fun."

He said, "No, Passion, there's no fun without you. Everything we have done throughout our lives, we have done together."

We get Passion loaded into the ambulance, and we get into our little trolley. They take us back to the reception area, where they tell us where they're taking Passion. We got to the hospital, and they took Passion in for an X-ray. It's confirmed that she broke her ankle and has three cracked ribs on the right side and two on the left. I did not realize she had fallen so hard. How could I have missed that? I guess because I was so focused on her ankle. I did not think to do a full assessment of her. I asked the doctor if she might have hit her head, and he replied, "We're going to do a full check-up on her to make sure. She does have a little bruise on her forehead, but we need to make sure she doesn't have a concussion. I'm sure she's going to be OK. She's in good hands."

"Thank you, sir."

Passion spends two weeks in the hospital. She has surgery to reconstruct her ankle enough so we can return home. It's going to be a long flight. We had booked our flights in economy class, but due to Passion's condition, they accommodated her by putting her in first class, where she could sit in a recliner and elevate her foot. The flight attendants and the captain were very attentive to her needs. I was very impressed by how they made us feel comfortable despite the accident. They told us that if we needed anything, we should let them know.

Finally, the flight takes off. We're heading home. It's a long flight that seems to take forever, but we make it home. We got our luggage, and Paul and Jenny got their car from the garage. Paul said, "Gabriel, do not worry about it. You can come to ride with me to get your car, and Jenny can stay with Passion until you get back. We can follow you back down and ensure we all do it back down."

"Oh, that would be wonderful. Thank you so much."

"Sure, Paul. Thank you, Jenny. Tell Jenny I said thank you, too. We're going to be OK."

Gabriel and I make it back to our car and head home. He asked me, "Passion, I'm so sorry about what happened to you."

"Oh, stop that, Gabriel. It wasn't your fault. I had an accident; it can happen to anybody. But I'm OK. I may have a long recovery ahead of me, but through it all, when I saw all that beauty up there and all that greenery, it took away a lot of the pain. I had the opportunity to see something I've never seen before, and I still say it was well worth it. If I had a chance to do it again, I would. We just need to be very careful because you never know what you could step off into."

"Well, Passion, if you feel that way, then it was worth it. We do not know how long your recovery is going to take. We'll just take it one day at a time."

"OK, Gabriel, we'll do that."

"Gabriel?"

"Yes, Passion?"

"If we do not get a chance to come back here next year, can we also travel somewhere else?"

"Sure, Passion. Wherever you want to go. Time is all we have. But first, we need to get you well before considering another trip. No matter where we go, it all depends on how you heal."

"I understand, Gabriel. One day at a time."

"Well, I know we like taking our showers together, Passion, but this time, it's going to be a little different. I'm going to take care of you. I will wash you up, get your pajamas on, and tuck you into bed. Then I will take a shower and join you in bed, just to hold you and show you that you are going to be OK."

"Oh, I like that. When you tell me that, it just makes me feel so good. Despite all the pain I may be in, you make it feel so much better. I noticed the doctor did not give you much pain medication. Just in case you have pain, do you think you are going to need any more tomorrow?"

"Oh, Gabriel, I just do not want to be taking all that medication. I understand you do not want me to be in pain, but it's not much. It's just that every once in a while, it starts to throb when my foot is hanging down. But as long as I keep my foot elevated, it's not bad at all."

"OK, then that is what we'll do. Let me get extra pillows so you can raise your foot."

"Thank you."

"No problem, sweetheart. Anything to make you feel comfortable. Come on, let us close our eyes and get some sleep. I will wait until the morning to see how you are feeling. Everything is still fresh, and you may feel a little different in the morning, but you are going to feel everything."

"Yes, Gabriel, I guess you are right. I will. Goodnight."

"Goodnight, Passion. I love you."

"I know, but I love you more, Passion."

JOY AND HOPE OF MY TOMORROW

*W*aking up this morning with so much joy in my heart, covered in the embrace of love from Gabriel, I know it won't be an easy road to recovery from my injury. One thing is for sure: I pray and ask God to ease the pain of today and all my tomorrows.

I move from Gabriel's embrace only to feel the full impact of the pain I am enduring. I did not expect this, but I guess the impact of everything that has happened is really showing this morning. But I know I have the strength to pull through this.

"Gabriel."

"Yes, Passion?"

"I really feel it this morning."

"Oh, Passion, I knew you would feel this pain today. As I told you yesterday, your body was still in shock, and all the pain hadn't come yet. But together, we're going to get through this."

"I do not want to get up right now. I just want to lie here in your embrace. My body's all shaken up, but I know you are going to be there for me."

"You know I will, Passion. Just lay here for a while, OK? I will go and get you a cup of coffee and bring you breakfast in bed."

"No, Gabriel, I do not think I could eat anything right now."

"Passion, you have to put something in your stomach to take your medicine. It is not good for you to take meds on an empty stomach; it would just upset you. And you really do not want to cough with a sore stomach."

"OK. How will I manage to get washed up this morning?"

"Do not worry about that, Passion. I have it all taken care of. Do not cry; it is going to get better. I am going to always be here for you."

Gabriel brought me a light breakfast, a cup of coffee, and some orange juice.

"Eat as much as you can, but make sure you drink your orange juice. You have to stay hydrated."

"I will, Gabriel. I will do my best."

I finished my breakfast, taking in as much fluid as I could. I did not drink all my coffee, but I did drink half my orange juice and ate very little food. I think, for now, it is better than nothing.

"Passion, it is time for me to sit you up on the side of the bed so I can get you cleaned up."

"Oh, Gabriel, it hurts so bad."

"I know, Passion, but we've got to get through this. Now that you have food in your system take some pain meds to make it a little easier for you. Do you think it will help?"

"Yes, I believe it will help."

Gabriel begins to wash my face. As more tears run down, he gently wipes them away.

"Passion, sweetheart, I love you with all my heart. I understand your pain, but we have to go through a little pain to get to the healing part. We're going to do this one step at a time."

Finally, Gabriel finishes washing me up, puts clean clothes on me, and sets me up in the chair so he can fix the bed. I feel a little more comfortable sitting up in the chair, and I do not want to get back in bed right then.

"Gabriel, can you get the footrest for me to rest my ankle on? When it hangs down, it throbs in pain."

"Yes, Passion, I will get it for you. Anything to make you comfortable."

Finally, Gabriel finishes the bed and gets himself cleaned up. He sits on the side of the bed and begins to talk to me to take my mind off the pain I am enduring. We talked about our trip, our journey, and how much fun we had, trying not to dwell on the injuries. We had such a laugh, but I would not change that trip for anything in the world. I had the opportunity to see something that most people dream of doing at our age, and only very few get a chance to travel that high. I am grateful for just that little bit.

"Passion?"

"Yes, Gabriel?"

"I am going to work on getting you a wheelchair because one thing is certain: you are not going to be confined to the house. We're still going to do the things we always do, just at a slower pace. Do not worry about how you are going to get in and out of the car. I will pick you up, and we will take the wheelchair wherever we go. We just cannot give up."

"OK, Gabriel."

"Guess what? I can feel the pain easing up on my ankle. It is not too bad, but when I cough or try to yawn a little bit, I can feel it in my ribs. I guess it is because they were cracked. If only I could stand up long enough to walk over to the window and see the birds in the garden."

"Passion, If I had a wheelchair, I could wheel you over there."

"Yeah, but Gabriel, the pain in my ribs. I will just wait until I am able to go downstairs. It is going to be a challenge."

"Passion, you did not just break your ankle in one spot; you broke it in several spots. Your big bone has a small fracture as well. The only reason they could not put a cast up that far was because your leg was so swollen by the time we got back home from our trip. But as soon as the swelling decreases, they will cast a full cast on you."

"I am going to talk to a few friends of mine who deal with lift chairs and see about having a lift put in the house so you can come up and down without worrying about how you will get down the stairs. I think this will be a plus for you, and you won't feel so isolated and helpless."

"OK, Gabriel. You know you are such a wonderful husband, so attentive to my needs. It is like I do not have to ask you for anything; you see it and act upon it. I guess we've been together for so many years that we know each other's feelings and the things we need to comfort us through our pain and joy."

"I just know that I want to be here for you, Passion. You are going to have good days and bad days, but through it all, we have to rely on our strength to pull you through it. We're not going to spend our days dwelling on the accident; we're looking forward to what our next adventure will be. It gives us something to look forward to. One thing is for sure: we need to start visiting more of the kids and the grandkids. Have fun doing things with them, take them to the amusement park, and watch them just laugh and enjoy themselves."

"I would love that, Gabriel."

"You know, we've been so blessed to watch our children grow to become parents themselves. What I enjoyed the most were the sounds of their cries and the moments of holding them in my arms, letting them know they were safe. You were a wonderful mother. You still are. Even as our children are grown, you have this thing about you; no matter how old they are, they still call you mommy and say her mom. That is their way of connecting with you. Hearing my daughter say, Daddy, you know that. We have so many memories of our children from school age to how they became adults, having their own opinions about things. Most of all, no matter how old they got, they always maintained a level of respect for us as their parents. Even when other children do things that would get under their parents' skin, we taught our children very well. As soon as you are able to travel, we're not going to let this injury stop us. We're going to visit them. We need that, and I am sure they will enjoy that as well."

"That would be wonderful, Gabriel. I just wonder how long it is going to take my ribs to heal because they really hurt when I cough."

"PASSION, with time, you'll move past this. The pain will fade, but you need to remind yourself every day that things will improve. Keep pushing forward, even though I know it won't be easy. Remember the saying: healing doesn't come without pain. You're an incredibly strong woman."

"Well, when you get some time, Gabriel, why don't we just sit back and write down the things we want to do and the places we want to go? We can try to map out a calendar so we have things to look forward to. It is just setting goals for ourselves."

"OK, Passion, we can do that. Let's shoot for maybe six months from now. It shouldn't stop us even if you are still in a cast. We will have a wheelchair to get around. I cannot wait to see the expression on the grandkids' faces when they see us. Our son has grown into a handsome young man with a beautiful wife. Even though he's living in that cold state of Montana, we will get past that. Maybe we can make that trip when the weather's not so bad. At our age, that cold air will not be agreeable to us."

"We really have to plan it out very carefully."

"OK, that is enough of that. I must run to the store to pick up a few things. Do you think you will be OK?"

"Yes, Gabriel, I will be fine. Please take your time to get whatever you need to get done."

"Is there anything in particular you would like me to pick up from the store while I am out?"

"Oh yes. I wrote out a list and need you to pick up a few things for me. Look at the list and see if I missed anything. I remember before we went on our journey to the mountains, I had started a list but never completed it."

"Oh, I know what you forgot."

"What's that, Gabriel?"

"You forgot my brand of cereal that I like."

"I sure did. Also, I wanted to change the type of milk we use because it kind of messes with my stomach. Maybe we could try oat milk; I hear it is really good for you and tastes great."

"OK, we could try that."

"Gabriel, when I am able to make it down the stairs, do you think we can get a high enough chair where I can sit and do some baking? I would love to make a fresh loaf of banana bread the way you like it. I just do not want to feel like I cannot do anything for myself."

"Yes, I understand that, Passion. But I told you, one day at a time. You will get a chance to make banana bread, but there's no hurry right now. I just want to get you over the rough part of this, where your pain is manageable. I do not want you to do too much right now."

"OK, Gabriel, you know what's best for me."

"Oh, by the way, Passion, do you remember me telling you I was going to stop by one of my friends about putting a lift in the house?"

"Yes, Gabriel, I remember."

"Well, on my way back from the store, or maybe before I go, I will stop by his place and talk to him about coming out to the house to measure our steps and see how much it is going to cost."

"OK, that would be great. If it seems like I am taking a little longer, just know what I am trying to take care of."

"I understand."

Three hours have passed. I did a little shopping for Passion and made it back home. Yelling to my wife, "Passion, I am back, sweetheart. I have taken care of everything I needed to. I did the shopping and stopped by a friend of mine about the lift."

"Oh great, are they able to do it?"

"Yes, and I explained to him what had happened. He told me not to worry; he would stop by later today to give us an estimate. I also told him I do not care how much it costs; I just need it so you can go up and down the stairs whenever you want. He'll be by today."

"OK, thank you so much, Gabriel."

"In the meantime, if you are able to do it, maybe you can sit, going down the stairs, one step at a time. You've been talking about wanting to see the birds. We have a chair with wheels on it. It may not be a wheelchair, but it has wheels. I could get you close to the window where you can see the birds. It is something better than nothing, so you do not have to stay upstairs all this time waiting."

"OK, Gabriel, that would be great."

"Knock, who's at our door right now?"

"I do not know, Passion. Let me go and check."

I opened the door, and to my surprise, the health care center delivered the wheelchair for you. I forgot that the doctor had ordered one for you, but I wasn't sure when it was going to come. It is here now. I am really happy because now you can scoot downstairs and sit in the wheelchair. I can take you outside to the garden where you always wanted to go to watch your birds."

"Oh baby, I am so happy."

"Now, you can try making the banana bread if you feel up to it. I will set up a nice board across the wheelchair's arms and bring the hand mixer over to you. You can make whatever you want."

"I would love that. It makes me feel like I am doing something and not just sitting around. It will take my mind off what I have been going through these last few days."

"OK, I will get everything you need—the bowl, the flour, and everything else. Just tell me what you need, and I will bring it to you one by one."

Finally, I finished mixing the banana bread and putting it in the pan. It is ready for the oven.

"Gabriel, did you preheat the oven for me?"

"Already done, Passion."

"OK, it is ready for the oven."

"I will put it in."

It has been 45 minutes.

"Gabriel."

"Yes, sweetheart, what is it?"

"The banana bread is ready to come out of the oven."

"OK, sweetheart, I will get it out for you."

"Wow, this looks good! I know it is going to be delicious."

"Let it cool down first before you can have any of it."

"I know, but it just smells so good."

"So now that you have made something for us to eat while sitting in your wheelchair for the first time, how does it feel being a little bit more mobile?"

"It feels wonderful that I am not just isolated upstairs."

"That is great. Anything to make you feel happy and comfortable in your condition. Have you talked to any of the kids to let them know what happened on our journey?"

"No, Passion, I did not talk to them. I did not want to get them all upset and worried. We've got this; we will make it through. They do not need to rush here to see us or check on you right now when everything's OK. Once it is all over, we can tell them about our journey and the good times, not focusing on the negative stuff that happened. I am sure we're not the only ones who have gone on a trip and had an accident. I just do not want to worry the kids."

"OK, that makes sense."

"Well, since you are downstairs, would you like to watch a movie or something on TV? Even though you are in a wheelchair, you do not have just to sit there. You can be on the couch as well. I can lift you up and put you on the couch."

"Gabriel, no, that is too much for you. I think if you put me close enough to the couch, I can scoot myself over. I do have one good leg, you know."

"Oh yeah, I forgot. I am just so attentive to you that I do not want you to go out of your way or feel any pain."

"Oh, stop that, Gabriel. I can help myself, too."

"OK, decide what you want to watch."

"Maybe let us watch a little western movie. I like that. I do not want to watch anything too dramatic."

"Passion, do you think the bread is cooled down enough for us to have a slice with a cup of coffee? It has been about 15-20 minutes; it should be cool enough but still warm."

"We could have a slice of that and a cup of coffee."

"Oh, that would be great, Gabriel."

"OK, I will go into the kitchen, remove it from the pan, and cut it."

"Oh, Passion, this bread is so scrumptious! My goodness, you really put your hand into this one. This is really good."

"Yes, it is very good. Come on, sweetheart, let us finish our bread and coffee and watch our movie."

"Well, that was a good movie. Do you want to sit down here for a while before we go back upstairs?"

"Yes, Gabriel, I'd rather sit here for a while. Maybe I can just lie back on the couch and prop up my leg. I could just stay down here until it is time to turn in for the evening."

"You know, Passion, that is a great idea. You have always taken care of me, and now it is my time to take care of you. I am going to prepare lunch for us today. Is there anything that you would like to have?"

"Well, not at this moment, but I am sure it will probably be something light, maybe a bowl of soup or salad."

"OK, either one. We have both, so just let me know."

"OK, I will."

THE QUEST FOR HOPE

"*P*assion, now that you have had something in your stomach, you need to take your meds. OK, I am going to run upstairs, get them for you, and bring them down. I will also get you some extra pillows so you can get more comfortable and let the medication kick in."

"Let me get you something to drink to take your medication. OK, here you go, sweetheart. Here's your pain med."

"Thank you."

"I want you to lie on this couch and relax. If you fall asleep, it is OK. I am going to take care of a few things around the house, and I will peak in now and then to check on you. If you need anything, let me know."

"OK, Gabriel, I am sure I will be OK. You just go ahead and do what you need to do."

Finally, waking up from a long nap, the house smells so fresh. Gabriel must have opened the windows. The fresh air smells so good. I am glad I am downstairs. Let me see if I can get into my wheelchair without calling Gabriel. I want to show him that I can help myself. I have to be careful because I do not want him to fuss at me for not asking for help.

Oh wow, look at me; I have managed to do it all by myself! Gabriel is going to be surprised. I heard him coming down the hallway.

"Passion, what did you do? Why didn't you call me?"

"Oh, Gabriel, stop that. I had to see what I could do for myself. You cannot do everything for me. You have to let me do some things on my own."

"I know, but I am just so afraid that you might fall and hurt yourself."

"Gabriel, allow me to do things for myself. Trust me, if I need your support getting into the wheelchair, I will call you."

"OK, Passion, I am just so afraid of your falling."

"It is OK, Gabriel, that's understandable. What's for lunch?"

"Well, do you want soup or salad?"

"I think I would have a bowl of soup."

"I figured you would say that, Passion. Because while you were asleep and I was doing chores, I made some homemade vegetable soup."

"You did? You did that for me?"

"Yes, Passion, I did it for both of us. The salad sounded good, but not as good as the soup with bread and butter."

"Well, since you have done that, let's just go ahead and have lunch. You know the wheelchair can roll underneath the table as well?"

"It will?"

"Yes, Passion, I can wheel you right up to the kitchen table, and we can sit and have lunch together. This is wonderful. What would you like to drink?"

"Can I have a cold glass of orange juice?"

"Sure, what else would you like?"

"Maybe a glass of water as well. I remember the doctor telling me to drink plenty of water."

"OK."

"Umm, the soup tastes so good. Are you sure you made this, Gabriel?"

"Yes, Passion, I made it. Whatever you put in it sure is good. Have you forgotten that I can cook, too?"

"Of course not. You see, now it is my time to cook and serve you."

"OK, well then, I can't wait to see what you're going to make for dinner."

"I have also prepared that while you were sleeping."

"OK, I will let you surprise me."

"You are definitely going to be surprised. You know, all we have is time with each other now."

"You know, Passion, taking care of all the chores in the house, the cooking, and cleaning, I did not realize how much work goes into accomplishing all these tasks daily. It is a lot for women; they have the strength to surpass anything a man could ever do. To master this, I commend you for a job well done. Even though everything we've done, we've done together in the house, seeing it at this level, I appreciate you more. I watched you lie on the couch, sleeping and resting, and I was saying to myself, 'This is one strong woman to do all these things and still have a smile on her face.' From this point on, we do all of this together."

Finally, we finish lunch, and everything is cleaned up.

"Passion, what would you like to do now?"

"Well, I definitely do not want to lie back down again. Do you feel like taking me outside in the wheelchair?"

"Sure, that is not a problem. The sun is out; it is a beautiful day, and it would be good for both of us."

"Gabriel, do you think we could go to the park?"

"What Park is that, Passion?"

"You know, we always go to the park and have a picnic lunch."

"Oh, I know which one you are talking about. Sure, we do not need to pack lunch. I just want to go there and walk around while you push me in the wheelchair."

"OK, we could do that. Let me grab a few things, grab my keys, and I will get the car out of the garage and take you there."

"OK, Gabriel?"

"Yes?"

"I love you."

"I know, Passion, and I love you too. Come on, let me get you loaded into the car and put the wheelchair in the trunk."

Finally, we made it to the park. Gabriel gets the wheelchair out of the car, and we start our walk in the park.

"Do you hear that, Passion?"

"What's that, Gabriel?"

"The children laughing and playing, swinging on the swings and playing on the seesaw. It reminds me of our children when they were small."

"I know; it is such a wonderful feeling and a beautiful sight to see. It makes me feel so warm inside because they're happy places. This is where I wanted to come; it brings back so many fond memories."

"Do you remember, even before we had our children, we used to come here ourselves? We would spread out a tablecloth on the grass, have a little lunch, and just enjoy ourselves."

"Yes, I remember."

"How long would you like to stay at the park, Passion?"

"Not too long, but long enough to enjoy it."

"OK, we won't stay too long because I want to get back to the house and prep for dinner."

"OK, but on our way back to the house, do you think we could stop and get an ice cream cone like we used to do?"

"Sure, if that is what you want, it is not a problem. There will be enough time between, so it doesn't affect your dinner."

"It won't affect my dinner, Gabriel."

"Wait, Gabriel, where are you going?"

"Hold on, Passion, I will be right back."

"Where did you find these?"

"You mean the flowers?"

"Yes, where did you find them? I did not see anyone walking around with flowers."

"Passion, it is because I turned your chair around so you would not see them. You know I can never pass up flowers for you. To set aside all your pain and come outside, wanting to go to the park, I had to get you something beautiful to make you feel even better. It is just a token of my love for you. Every girl deserves flowers through her good times, bad times, pain, and happiness."

We finally made it back to the car. Gabriel lifted me inside and put the wheelchair back in the trunk. We're heading to the ice cream parlor for an ice cream cone.

"Gabriel, you remember what my favorite ice cream cone was, don't you?"

"Come on, Passion, how could I ever forget? You always say the rainbow gives you a taste of all the flavors. How could I ever forget this? You have had the same taste since we were young, playing as little kids. You have never changed that. I can say you have been consistent in the kind of ice cream you want."

"Gabriel, aren't you going to get one as well?"

"Yes, I will. I will get my favorite one, too."

"Great. Let's just eat it and hurry home so you can prepare everything for dinner." "OK, we finally made it back to the house. We will unload and get back inside." To my surprise, there's a table spread set up just for us.

"Gabriel, what did you do? Who did this?"

"Oh, Passion, do not worry about all of that. It is something I prepared especially for you. When you asked me about going to the park, I thought this would be the perfect time to set things up. Remember me telling you about dinner and that I had everything planned? Well, I hired a private chef to prepare dinner for us."

"Stop, Gabriel, you are about to make me cry. I have flowers, and there are flowers on the table, too?"

"Yes, Passion, there are. You can never have too many flowers. Come on, I am going to take you to the bathroom so you can freshen up. This is why I wanted you to wear this special dress; I had everything set up."

"Yes, Passion, I did."

Finally, we sat down at the table and had our dinner.

"Gabriel, this is such a beautiful spread. The food looks so good. I know you prepared something very special for both of us, something I know we are going to enjoy."

"I am sure it is going to be very good. Would you like a glass of wine?"

"Sure, that would be wonderful."

"Wow, Gabriel, this is nice. I love the taste of this. This must be a nice French wine because it is something I have never tasted before. Even though I am familiar with other brands, this taste is extraordinary. I know you will like it, Passion. This is why I selected this one, and the chef made a good suggestion on this one as well. Let us have a toast."

"OK, that sounds good. What would you like to toast to?"

"Let us toast to happier times and the continuation of our love for one another."

"That sounds beautiful. OK, let's go ahead and eat."

"Passion, what do you think about the sauce that he created for us?"

"I love it. Yes, it is really good. The hollandaise on the salmon is just wonderful, and on the asparagus as well. What can I say? It is a beautiful meal. Thank you so much, Gabriel. This really means a lot to me."

Finally, we finished our meal, and it was about time to turn in for the evening.

"Gabriel, do you want dessert?"

No, I'm full from dinner."

"That is no problem. We could have it later on this evening, maybe after we've had our showers."

"That sounds like a good idea."

"So, Passion, how do you feel about the lift I had installed in the home? It is temporary; they must help you up and down the stairs. Once you finish therapy, you can have it removed.

"I really love it because it makes me feel like I have my independence back again. I do not have to rely on you to do everything to get me up and down. I can do it. It may take a little while, but I know I can make it through. Gabriel, you are such a wonderful husband, and I thank God every day for you and bless Him for the things that you do for me. You know, it is funny how you look back on life and feel as if you are the only two living in this world because you are so focused on your marriage. When two people love each other so deeply, you do not think about anybody else but yourselves. It is not that you exclude yourself from the world of people; it is just that when you focus on a marriage, you do not think about anything coming in to disrupt that. We just hold on to each other's hands and continue."

"OK, are you ready to go upstairs now so we can get our showers and stuff and get ready?"

"I think we will have our desserts upstairs instead of going all the way back downstairs. This way, we could sit by the bed next to the fireplace and enjoy ourselves."

"OK, Passion, that sounds like a good idea. Do you need any help getting into the shower?"

"No, I think I can manage this one this time but thank you."

"I will stand by and make sure you do not fall."

"OK, Gabriel."

I made it into the shower, and Gabriel followed as he had always done.

"Come on, sweetheart, let me wash your back for you."

"OK, and I will wash your back too."

"Be careful not to put too much pressure on that foot."

"I won't. I will hold on to the bar."

"I will. Thank you, Gabriel."

"You are welcome, sweetheart."

Finally, I got out of the shower, and Gabriel came out behind me. We continued to dry each other off as we always have. We got into our nighties, and I got back on my chair. Gabriel wheeled me back into the bedroom where the fireplace was going. It was so warm, and the atmosphere felt so good. Who would ever think that a bedroom could be a place of solace? Even though downstairs is just as beautiful, it is so warm and cozy here.

Finally, we had our dessert. Gabriel summoned the chef to let him know we would have our dessert in our bedroom. To our surprise, when he opened the lid, there was a beautiful slice of coconut cake, my favorite, a cup of coffee with goat milk that I like, and what do you know, a single rose. The night was drawing near. We finished our dessert, got tucked into bed, and said, "Sweet dreams until tomorrow morning."

It is a new day, and the morning has come. I'm not sure what to expect, but it has to be great.

"Gabriel, are you awake?"

"Sure, Passion, I am awake."

"I would like to try something different this morning."

"What is that?"

"I want to use my crutches to make it to the bathroom on my own. Would you stand behind me, guide me, and make sure I do not fall in case I get weak?"

"Sure, no problem."

As I began to walk with the crutches, I realized I was putting more pressure on my foot, just like my therapist said I would. I knew I would end up doing that when the time was right, but I was told not to overdo it. I guess my fears had consumed me because I was afraid to take this step. But today is a new day, and I must push myself to improve. My legs are still a little tender, but I can work with that to have both my feet available for walking again.

"I made it to the bathroom alone, and I wanted to shower alone, but Gabriel did not have that.

"Well, you know, Passion, we've always taken showers together, and that is not going to change."

"OK, Gabriel, come on in."

We did our usual shower routine, and we got out. I made it out all by myself. I cannot believe it. I did it! Finally, I am so happy because this day is truly an accomplishment for me.

"Gabriel?"

"Yes, Passion."

"I am going to be alright. I can see the light beyond the shadow."

In the days following this morning, I continued to get better and better to the point where I did not need the wheelchair, the crutches, or the cane. I was walking with just a small limp. God is good, and I thank Him every day of my life for giving me the courage to move forward despite all the pain I endured. But I must say, I would do it all over again because, despite all my injuries, that trip will last me a lifetime. I had so much fun, and it was worth it.

"Gabriel, I do not want the children to know anything about this accident, so I hope you did not call them and tell them what happened to me. We do not need to worry them."

"No, Passion, I did not call them. I felt like if you wanted them to know, it was your story to tell."

"Gabriel, do you think it will be OK for me to walk outside the garden, smell the fresh flowers, and look at the birds? You know that is my pastime, and I enjoy it so much. And look at me; I am walking again. I am not held in bondage by artificial support, but I am walking on my own. And I know there's you, my watchful eye. I love you so much, Gabriel. I do not know what I would do without you."

"Oh, there you go again, Passion. I am going to always be there for you until I take my last breath."

"Passion, you used to say this to me every morning. I was your joy when you woke up in the morning. I am going to take it a step further because, to me, you are my joy. When I look into your face, you are the beat in my heart; you are my safe place when we're lost, and most of all, you are my happiness."

"Oh, wow, Gabriel, that is so beautiful and so very well-spoken."

"Look at us now, comforting souls with all our hearts." Gabriel, I am feeling a bit weak and tired, and I would love to rest a little bit.

I called Saida and Jabril to see how they were doing. They said everyone was doing great. As they had mentioned before, the grand-kids are growing so tall. I just miss them so much. Saida told me, "Momma, I have a conference I must attend. And hopefully, if I get a chance to get away, I will be coming to see you and Daddy. I have a babysitter for the kids, and she is making sure the kids get to school while I am away for these few days."

"Oh, Saida, I cannot wait to see you."

"Me too, momma."

MOMMA

Mamma, that is me on the other side of your bedside table, watching over you as you sleep. I want to thank you for teaching me how to love unconditionally, to love with embrace and intent. I never knew what it was like to be without love, especially coming from a mother. There was never a time that I went hungry or that there was no food to fill my belly because you always made a way. It may not have always been what we wanted, but our bodies needed it.

I think so much about my childhood, the way we played, and how you were always there for us. We saw so many children go home without their mothers and fathers being there, but you were always there for us because you lived your life for us, your little dolls, as you would call us. As I see where my life is now, I just want to say, Mama, thank you for molding me into the woman I am today. I do not know how to display hate because it was never given, and sometimes, hate can be blinded because we are so focused on the love we receive. It never came into our lives, so it was easy for us to receive love.

I remember all the time you would walk us to the park, Mom, and you would push us one by one on the swing set. We would just laugh out loud and be happy because we had our mom. We always wished we had our own swing set so we wouldn't have to take those long walks to the park, but we cherished those moments. The most important thing, Mama, is that you took turns holding each of our hands, making us feel loved and needed. Of course, we all wanted more love from you than the other, but you always told us that you loved no one more than the other. And we would play games with you, creating memories that I hold dear to this day.

I sit back, Mom, and reminisce so much about all those good times we had more good times than bad, Mama. We always came together as a family and never allowed anyone to overshadow that. People looked down on us because we did not have much, but they did not realize we had more than they did because we had our mother's love. You were always there for us. A lot of kids come home to an empty house with no mother or father, just four walls, wondering what they're going to eat.

Mommy, you always told us to make sure that we kept a seed, at least one bean, in our pockets. You said that if we ever got lost in the woods, we could grow that seed and have the vegetables we needed to fill our stomachs. You taught us to learn about different trees, to peel back the bark and dig up the roots because there were nutrients in them. You taught us about all the different herbs that would heal us in case we got sick in the woods, what each leaf meant, and what it was supposed to do for us. I cannot forget those times because those lessons still resonate with me today.

We grew up in such a religious family, and I know one day, we will all grow up and move away. We always wondered what you would do with your life because you spent so much of it by yourself. I get it now: your loneliness did not consume you because you were very creative, and with that creative mind, you found things to do.

Mama, you remember how we used to sit on the porch and watch all those children swinging on the swing sets, playing hopscotch, and going about their daily lives. We always hoped to hear those sounds again the next day. And I know as you got older, loneliness became your best friend.

I sit at home every day and night and wonder what you have done throughout your day. I cannot remove my emotions from this equation because it is the element of how I feel when my shoes become the soles of my feet. But you have walked in your shoes for many years. Do you know where your journey took you? You have to tell me—hold your head high to the sky and let it guide you. Look at the beauty through your eyes, for it is then that you will see.

Mama, I know we cannot fly, but we can run and keep on running. But when it is all done, sometimes we realize that we never truly get to where we're going because we never allowed the doors to open and close slowly enough to absorb what we have learned. But I have learned so much. When opening books, we never finish chapters without a title; we tell ourselves we know it all. That was me, Mama, because I felt as if there was nothing more to be learned from all that you had taught me, but I felt like I knew it all.

I learned that things do have challenges, and those challenges give us the motivation to do better. Yes, I've fallen many times in my life, but none kept me down. I learned through life that the only person who can pick me up is myself.

Mama, as I see you sleeping there beside me, as I am feeling before you, I know you hear me, and I know you want to say something back to me, but your presence speaks to me. It lets me know that you have taught me well, but I'll always be by your side, Mama, till the end.

It is funny how life is. Sitting back, thinking that when we were children, our mother would never leave us, we've learned as we've gotten older that you cannot have life without death. But I just do not want to talk about death because I want to sit back and reminisce about all those good times we had, Mama. I am half-paying and hoping that God will allow us to have more.

Mama, can you squeeze my hand and let me know that you are there? Oh, thank you, Mama. You are still there, listening to me? Go on, you used to say that all the time. You have so many words and so many things to say. Do you ever stop talking? No, Mama, I cannot because there is so much to be said to you. It is the idea and the feeling of knowing that I can say the word "Mama" over and over. My biggest fear is that a time will come when I cannot repeat those words in this life. I am having a problem with that one.

I am so glad I had the opportunity to be with you, even though you cannot talk to me. But you hear me, and you feel me, and I can touch you and feel the warmth from your hand, letting me know that you hear me. I'll always be by your side, Mama.

I have a story, Mama, that I am going to talk to you about today. I took a journey back into my own path just to become who I am today, going through what I experienced and becoming wiser from my mistakes. I've stumbled on many walks in my path, but none kept me down, even though sometimes the rocks would get bigger, making my steps much higher.

If only they knew that not even a wall too high or a river too wide could stop my struggle for happiness and fulfillment. I've had my share of ups and downs, but nothing pushed me to give up. For sure, Mama, for myself, it is about to come to an end.

One cool night in September, tucked away, I decided to take a walk to clear my thoughts and figure out my life. As I was walking and traveling on this dark and lonely road, I stopped for a moment, only to realize that I was at the forest entrance, as if someone or something had led me there. It was so peaceful and calm. My mind was traveling in so many different directions, trying to grasp what was about to unfold.

As I continued to walk to the entrance of this beautiful forest, I looked to the ground and saw all these beautiful creatures roaming the forest floor, going about their daily lives. The further I walked, the more the forest began to open for me, opening my thoughts. All of a sudden, I looked behind me and saw these small creatures following me: squirrels and chipmunks. Some were in front, and some were in the back of me as if they were waiting for me. Some were carrying nuts and berries. Others were just roaming the forest carrying their babies on their backs. With food also in their mouths. I can hear many different birds chirping. Not sure what this is all about. I hope it is a welcoming melody. It was like the forest had welcomed me into its world of many things to be seen. The sun was starting to go down, and it would be getting darker soon. I knew I wouldn't make it back to the forest entrance in time, so I just continued on my journey.

Being so deep in the forest, my mind was free to think, with burdens off my shoulders—or at least I thought so. I spotted a large figure in the shadow to my left. As I took a few more steps, I saw that it was a black bear. Sweat ran down my face, not knowing what I was going to do next. I looked to my right, and there stood another bear. At that moment, I felt like I might not make it out alive.

They did not attack but just walked along each side of me, guiding me. It was dark now, and I was hungry and tired. I reached a small pond where there was a tree stump, and I sat down beside it. The squirrels that had been traveling with me for some time were dropping nuts and berries for me to eat. I ate as if it was going to be my last meal. I knew it wasn't going to be my last meal because, deep down, I knew nothing bad would happen to me; I had faith in the man above.

You taught me so much in this harsh world. Are you still with me? Squeeze my hand again. Oh, you are still there. I thought you had fallen asleep. I have so much I want to talk to you about. My mind is racing, and I know this is the only way to talk to you. You can just listen and reflect on our childhood, how we grew up, and the things we did as we got older.

In the theological world we live in today, a mother's love is celebrated on a special day set aside to honor her suffering for the children she bore. It is an indescribable pain that no man can comprehend. Yet, as she brings forth a child into the world, she's able to stand just after giving birth, enduring insurmountable pain. Man has set aside this special day called Mother's Day, but we all know that every morning, noon, and night is Mother's Day. She cooks, washes dirty clothes and dishes, mops the floor, prepares the kids for their bath, and puts them to bed. She is the first to wake up in the morning and the last to lay her head down at night. Mama, good God almighty, the power of a woman, a mother beyond mothers.

Sometimes, when I miss you so much, I look at your picture just to hear your voice. I take it to the mirror and put it next to my face. How could I ever forget that face? I am a mirror reflection of you. I started talking to it, just as if you were there next to me. You always said that when your time comes, I should take that picture and place it in the mirror.

Mama, the treasure chest I have is where I keep all my childhood memories. Do you remember when you took me to the doctor because I fell and hurt my knee badly? You held me so tight and said, 'Baby, it is going to be alright.' The doctor told me to be careful next time. I was so happy, Mama, because I had you to myself. When we got back to the house, I did not care who grabbed you first because you had given me so much of your time and love that I was satisfied. Mama, there are so many memories. I cannot read all of the pictures or tell the story of each one in the chest. Old and new, they hold and keep the memories alive.

I lay here, Mama, and look at you, a strong woman never giving up, never bowing down to anyone. Your strength has carried you so far, and even when people look down on you, you still hold your head up high. I do not believe there is a mountain high enough for you to go above. You have the ability and compassion to love even those who do not love you. When you can do that, so can your children. It is like saying, let us not spend a lifetime wondering what people owe us. Do the best you can for the world and put your stamp on it. I know I am relying on you, Mama, but I have so much on my mind, so much I want to say.

I know that you have an internal influence over me. That is what defines you. If someone were to ask me today to define motherhood, I do not believe there is enough paper for me to write it on. I keep telling myself that mothers are a very special breed of people. She's the healer of her children, the nurse who cools their fevers, the medicine maker when you cannot afford to go to the doctor, the chiropractor when our legs and back hurt so much, the handkerchief that wipes away our tears, the teacher of things we do not understand. But most of all, Mama, she has everything in one package.

Who would have known they would never leave my side during the night? Those two bears stood out there, watching me. Would I become their meal? As if I could see them from a distance, I started to drift off to sleep, unaware that I might wake up to being eaten alive.

The next day came. I opened my eyes and realized I was still alive. Wondering if this was real, I looked around for the bears, not realizing they were lying beside me. They kept me warm throughout the night. After all that fear, they, too, had become watchers over me.

It was time for me to get up and try to find food to eat. I reached back into my bank of memories and used the survival skills my mother taught me as a child. I knew then I had friends in the forest, and I knew I was going to be okay. With all the trees, I looked for an oak tree. I started digging and pulling up the roots and used some water near the pond to clean and prepare my food for the morning. I could not forget about the little and big friends who had watched over me. They, too, needed something to eat. We all began to eat together.

It is getting late, Mama. It is time for me to go to bed. My mother turned her head over and looked at me. I was in shock. She called out my name. I said, "Mama?" She said, "Yes, Passion, it is me."

"You know, I listen to everything you say. That is what kept me focused —just to hear your voice. Your tone has the sound of a beating heart. It brought me out of this deep sleep. Come here, give me a hug."

"Passion, I am so proud of the woman you have become. I know that path wasn't very easy for you, but you took what you were taught and applied it to your life. And you made it yours. Now look at you, looking just like me. Passion, the doors will continue to open for you as long as you do not allow hate in your heart."

"I know, Mama. Can I ask you something?"

"Yes, Passion, what is it?"

"Well, now that you are awake, I have so many questions, and I know it is late."

"No, Passion, I am well rested. Talk to me. What's on your mind?"

"You raised me to have something to believe in, even when I did not believe in myself. You stood by me. You see, I've gone through things in my life, and I took on your strength to make it through the rough roads."

"Passion, get to what you want to talk to me about."

"You see, Mama, it was the day I started believing."

"Believing what, Passion?"

"It was a dream that I had, and it was so real."

"Ok, tell me about it."

"One day, I was traveling along this dark and lonely road. As I started to walk, I began to talk to myself, and I asked myself: What, when, where, and why. What do you mean by that? What did I ever do? When do I really start believing? Where do I find God again? Because you raised me to believe in him. Why did I suffer so much as I became a teenager?"

"As I continued to walk, listening to the birds chirping, the word "What" came to me. I looked to the sky and asked the man above, 'What did I do to deserve so many hardships in my life? When will you give me a sign to let me know you still exist? When will I find you again, the God everyone speaks so dearly about? Why did I have to suffer so much?'"

"As I started walking to find a quiet place to stop, look up, and talk to God, I found an open space in the woods by an old broken tree. I knelt on this wooden stump and started to have a conversation with God. I shouted out and prayed as if I had never prayed one day in my life, tears running down my cheeks. The air got so silent. Suddenly, this large gust of wind was tearing through the trees with a roar of thunder, as if God had opened heaven's doors and spread the forest to see me from down below. Mama, there stood this image of a man from heaven above."

"I became so afraid. Suddenly, something or someone wrapped their hands around me and held onto me tightly. It picked me up and whispered very softly. As he began to carry me and said these words: 'Child, oh my child, fear me not. I am going to hold you in my arms and talk with you. I have something I would like to explain to you.'"

"I see you grew up without many friends and feeling alone. Many have. But with all that said, you asked, what did you ever do to deserve such a hard adult life? Well, you see, Passion, I knew what I had in store for you when you were born. Your life was not so hard. I gave you challenges in life like I gave my son. He sacrificed his own life and died for you and many more."

"You have survived every death sentence man has bestowed upon you. You have always known me. Otherwise, how could you call out my name?"

"You asked, when did I start believing? Passion, in your precious heart, your conscience allows you to believe that all things are possible, and only through me when you believe."

"Passion, you asked where you find God. Little do you know, I've always been there, guiding your every step."

"Lastly, you asked me, Passion, why did you suffer so much? See, Passion, I knew you were one of my strong children who could withstand the storms of life. From the first blackened eye, the knife that cuts into your flesh, the falls that bruised your body, and the words that slice into your tender heart, bleeding to no end. I healed it. It was then, Passion, that I carried you."

"Mama, those were the questions I had for God. And after he talked to me, I had this sense of calm."

"Passion."

"Yes, Mama?"

"Turn around."

I looked and said, "Look at you, Mama. You are sitting up."

"Come over here. Never doubt for one moment that God doesn't hear you. I used to think and feel that way at one point in my life. But look where I am today. He has kept me and strengthened me throughout my life. And until my dying breath, I will always hold him in my heart. Thank you for listening to me."

"Can I get you something to eat or drink?"

"No, I just want to get up and look out of the window for a moment. Come here."

"Yes, Mama. What is it?"

"You see those trees over there?"

"Yes."

"Count them. How many did you count?"

"Ten."

"When you all grew up and left home, I planted trees for each son and flower bushes for all my girls. But one of them stood out more. I called that one 'Strength.' Because no matter what she was going through, she always found the strength to get back up. I go down and water every last one of them every chance I get."

"Hold on, momma, do you hear that?"

"No, what is it?"

"I hear Dad talking to someone. Let me go and see. Momma, it is Jabriel."

I ran to my brother and gave him the biggest hug.

"I missed you so much."

Dad yelled upstairs, "Passion, it is our son."

Jabriel dashed up the stairs into Momma's room. I followed right behind him. He just dropped to the floor and lay in momma's arms, like he did as a little child.

"Oh, Jabriel, I am so happy to see you. You and your sister surprised me. Look at you, a handsome young man."

"Oh, where are the kids?"

"Mom, I did not bring them because school was in session. I know you would have loved to see them. I promise to bring the whole family next time. You do not know how often I have looked at your and Dad's pictures. Our childhood, what fond memories."

"But why are you upstairs, Mom? Let us go downstairs."

"Well, son, I've been kind of under the weather and wasn't feeling good. I wasn't going to call you or your sister to let you know what was happening because I was sure I would get better." "So, how do you feel right now?"

"I am a lot better now."

"Well, do you feel like going downstairs?"

"I believe so."

"OK, I'll let Dad know that I am bringing you downstairs."

THE HEART THAT FUELED IT ALL

Over the last five years, a lot of time has passed since the beginning of our children's and grandchildren's lives, and we've enjoyed every moment of it.

"Gabriel, sometimes when you're sitting alone, what is the first thing that comes to your mind or your heart?"

"Passion, I think a lot about how we first met and how our children reminisced about those times. It is hard to say what the best times were because all of those were the best times, and I know we're going to have many more."

"There is something I've been wanting to talk to you about for quite some time, things that I've held to myself because I did not want you to worry, nor did I want the children to worry."

"What is it, Passion?"

"Do you remember the fall I had years ago when we went on vacation to climb up the mountains, and I broke my foot and ribs?"

"Yes, I remember that. It was so long ago, and you healed quite well from that."

"Well, that is not exactly true."

"What do you mean, Passion?"

"I've been having pain in my chest area where I had cracked the ribs. The pain comes and goes, but it just will not go away."

"Passion, why did you say anything about this? You could have had it checked out. How long has it been going on?"

"Well, it has been off and on for the last month, and I thought it would get better, but it is only getting worse."

"That is it. We're going back to the doctor again. You need to get another evaluation to see what's going on because that shouldn't hurt you unless something else happens. I am going to call the doctors and see if we can get an appointment for you."

"OK, Gabriel."

"Passion, I do not know what I would do if something happened to you. I am not ready to lose you, so please do not hold back or hide anything from me about how you're feeling or what's going on. I know you do not want to worry me, but you're my responsibility, and I do not want to see you in pain. You cannot suffer in silence like that, OK?"

"OK, Gabriel, I will not do that again. I will let you know what's going on with me."

"Thank you, Passion. But for right now, we're taking you to the doctor."

"I called the doctor's office today, and they gave me an appointment for you on Wednesday at 1:15. We're going. I do not care what else is going on, but we're going to make this appointment."

"OK, Gabriel."

"Come on, let us get tucked into bed."

"Well, first of all, we have our ritual."

"What is that, Passion?"

"We always take our showers together. We cannot change that."

"OK, not a problem. I wasn't sure if you were up to it, but we can do that. I will also bring your night clothes and my pajamas into the bathroom." Finally, we finished our showers and got tucked into bed. I still have this annoying pain around my ribs and chest area.

"Passion, I hear you moaning, sweetheart. Are you in some pain right now? Maybe we need to go to the emergency room."

"No, Gabriel, I can make it to my appointment tomorrow."

"Can I get you some aspirin or something to help you get through the night?"

"No, I am just going to try to lie a little differently tonight and hope it eases up a little bit."

"I am really afraid for you right now, Passion. I am not going to sleep tonight. I am going to watch over you."

"Gabriel, you do not need to do that. Just come back to bed and stay next to me. Just hold me through the night."

The morning is calm. I turned over to look at Gabriel, but he was not in bed with me. I wonder where he's at. All of a sudden, he came through the bedroom door with a cup of coffee and breakfast that he had made for us.

"Gabriel, I did not know you had left the bed."

"I know, Passion. You were sound asleep, and I did not want to wake you. I want you to rest. Anyway, I made breakfast for us. I want you to just lie in bed until it is time to get up and get ready for your noon appointment to see the doctor."

"But why are you crying, Gabriel?"

"Passion, do you realize how hard it is for me to watch you suffer in silence, and you never say a word to me? Only yesterday did I come to know about this, and now I feel your pain. We have to do something about it. I hope it is just a strained muscle or something, nothing serious."

"Come on, Gabriel, let us not think the worst. Let's wait until we see the doctor."

Finally, it is time to visit the doctor's office for my appointment. The nurse called me in. So, we both get up and follow the nurse into one of the examination rooms. We were just waiting for the doctor to come in so I could explain what was happening. Finally, he made it into the examination room, and I shared with him what I'd been experiencing and what was going on. He told me not to worry; they would do X-rays and some blood work to ensure everything was OK, and I should have some results by the next day. He asked me to hop up on the table so he could examine me. He checked my throat to ensure I did not have a sore throat, infection, or sinus infection. He checked the little cough that I had as well and checked my ears. My ears were clean; there was no buildup in there. When he went to rub down my chest area, I had a little pain there as his fingers started moving down my back and then my front chest area. He happened to feel a lump there.

He said, "Hmm, Passion, what is this?"

I said, "Doctor, I do not know what that is. It has been there for a while now, but this last week, it has gotten worse. That is why I am here today—I do not understand what's happening to me. I remember the fall I had years ago. I am not sure if this has anything to do with that or if it is a rib that never healed. I am really confused."

"Well, we really need to get that checked out," he said.

"You're not leaving right now. I am going to send you over to radiology to have them take a picture of this. We will get all these X-rays done and see what they show us. I also want to get some labs on you ASAP, okay?" the doctor said.

He asked me if I was in a hurry to get home, and I said no. Then I asked Gabriel, "Are we in a hurry to return home?" He said no.

He also said, "We're not leaving here until the doctor finds out exactly what's going on with you." That made me feel so good that he was so attentive to what was going on at that moment. I just could not bear the pain any longer. Gabriel and I headed over to radiology to get the X-rays and lab work done, and we came back to the office as soon as it was finished.

We got everything done. After we finished the X-rays and the lab work, we got something to eat. When we made it back to the doctor's office, we let the nurse know that we were back so she could summon the doctor. Immediately, he called us back.

The doctor had this strange look on his face. I looked at Gabriel, and Gabriel looked at me. We both said at the same time, "What's wrong?" The doctor dropped his head and said, "I want to do a little more study on what we found to make sure."

At this time, I was afraid. Gabriel asked me if I could wait in the waiting room for just 5 minutes so he could talk to the doctor. I said, "Sure, Gabriel, but why can't I be here when it is all about me?"

"Well, Passion, sometimes doctors can say things that we all do not understand. Since I've been in the medical field, I can explain things a little bit better for you if you do not understand once we get home," Gabriel explained.

"OK, I will wait. Doctor, can you please tell me what's going on with my wife? I know that looks all too well," Gabriel said.

"Gabriel, the X-rays show a large mass leading from her back to the front part of her rib cage. We do not know what that is, but it doesn't look good. I want to set her up for more in-depth testing. I want a CT scan done on her before I say anything," the doctor said.

"Come on, doctor, you've got to give me more than that. What does it indicate?" Gabriel insisted.

"It showed a large mass, the size of which I've never seen before. It must have been there for quite some time, growing without any indication of pain until now when it has become very serious," the doctor explained.

"Are you telling me I am going to lose my wife?" Gabriel asked.

"That is not what I am saying. We have big concerns. Just wait, and let us get all the testing done before we conclude what we have to work with," the doctor replied.

Finally, I returned to the room and asked the doctor and Gabriel if everything was okay. Gabriel had tears in his eyes, and I really thought something was wrong that they hadn't told me yet. Gabriel just got up and said, "Come on, sweetheart, let us go. The doctor will get back to us because he wants further testing done."

"Okay, but he's also going to give you a prescription for pain meds to help ease the pain a little bit," the doctor added.

We finally reached the car, and Gabriel asked me, "Are you okay, Sweetheart?"

"I am okay. Why do you keep asking me that?" I replied.

"Well, Passion, the pain is written all over your face. I am trying to do something to take that pain away. Whatever's going on in your body, I know you can fight this illness with the courage you have. You have encouraged me through challenging times of my sickness and stood strong even when I could see the teardrops on your chin. You always say, 'I am here, day by day, throughout the night.' Even when I lack the necessary courage while facing my fears, I ask God to just hold on to me," Passion said Gabriel. I am trying to steer away from that doubtful mind of self-pity. I am too strong for that; we all know self-pity is a senseless emotion. In this life, there is no suffering without pain… pain is the interceptor of suffering."

"Passion, it is still early in the day. Would you like to go to a movie? It is not like we have any other plans," Gabriel suggested.

"Really, Gabriel?"

"Yes, Passion."

"Oh, Gabriel, I would love that. We can get our popcorn and just enjoy the day with something positive," I said.

"Anything special showing?" I asked.

"I am not sure. We will have to wait until we get there to see what's showing, but something good. Nothing sad."

"Oh yes, that would be great. We've had enough sadness for today."

"I am so sorry, Gabriel. I have to go to the bathroom."

"Okay, let me hurry up and get parked."

"Okay, oh, finally, we made it into the theater. I will be right back, Gabriel."

"Okay, Passion. I will wait right here."

I finally returned to the lobby and saw Gabriel standing in line to get our popcorn and drinks.

"Did you figure out what movie we're going to see?" I asked.

"Yes, I did," Gabriel replied.

"Okay, and what is it called?"

"It is called 'When All Hopes and Dreams Are Possible.'"

"Wow, that is a good title. I wonder what it is all about."

"I am sure it will be good."

We finally got our snacks and went into the theater. The movie had already started. As we began to watch, we looked at each other, and it was like, "Gabriel, this movie is like an image of us. It is like we're the people in the movie."

"Quiet now, Passion. Let us just watch the movie and enjoy it."

Finally, the movie ended. Gabriel squeezed my hand, and we both stood up at the same time. We looked at each other, not knowing what to say, with tears still running down our faces. We got back in the car, and both said at the same time, "Did we just watch our life play on a large screen?"

I held my head down as Gabriel continued to drive out of the parking lot to head home. Finally, we arrived home. Gabriel came around and opened the door for me to let me out, and we went into the house. I proceeded to the living room to sit down for a bit.

Gabriel came over to me and said, "Passion, there is something I need to talk to you about that transpired at the doctor's office."

"Okay, what is it?"

"Do you remember when I asked you to step outside for a minute so I could talk with the doctor?"

"Yes, I remember that."

"Well, he said that when they received the X-rays back, it showed that you had a large mass coming from your back to the front of your chest wall, and it did not look good. Before he could tell me anything, he wanted to do more testing on you. He wanted to set you up for a CT scan."

"Okay, could it be maybe just an infection?"

"No, Passion. The way he was talking seemed to be a little bit more than that. Let us just hold back and wait. We will get a call from a radiologist when we can go in for the CT scan. In the meantime, let us not dwell on that right now. Let us just enjoy the moment, okay?"

"Gabriel, can you fix me a hot cup of coffee?"

"Sure, sweetheart. Anything you would like."

"I do not feel much up to eating dinner tonight."

"It is not a problem, but if you get hungry, just let me know, and I will fix something."

"Gabriel, come here for a second."

"Hold on, Passion."

"No, Gabriel, come here. What's going on? Why are you crying? Did I do something? Did I say something?"

"No, Passion, you did neither. It is just that I love you so much more than you realize, and the thought of something being wrong with you is tearing me up. You always told me to be strong through everything, any pain I was in. I am doing the best I can. I know my pain sometimes gets unbearable, but it has only been a week, Gabriel. Do not do that to me. Let me rely on my own strength. I need this for myself. We both need to remain positive."

The following morning, the radiology team called us and told us we had an appointment for the CT scan today at 3:15. We made it through the appointment, and they started the procedure. They had me take my clothes off and put on a gown. Then I lay on this bed, and my whole body went through what looked like a tunnel. I've never seen something so massive in my life, just for a CT scan. Finally, I was all done. They told me I could go in and get cleaned up and put my clothes back on. They were finished with what they had to do. They said they would be sending the test results to my doctor. From the first appointment up to now, three days later, I will return to my doctor again. At this time, Gabriel looked as if he weren't ready for any bad news, but we just waited.

The nurse called us back into the doctor's exam room. We waited about five minutes before the doctor finally came in and told us the news.

"Passion, the CT scan showed a large mass. I am not quite sure what it is, which is why I wanted to send you more testing to make sure. The CT scan showed a large mass that may be a tumor. I want to do a biopsy, and if it is a tumor, we want to go in and remove it," the doctor explained.

Gabriel asked the doctor if it was cancerous, but he could not answer that question just yet. He wanted us to go home, talk about it, and think about what we wanted to do.

"If it can be removed, we want it done as soon as possible," Gabriel insisted.

The doctor looked at me and asked, "Passion, how do you feel about this?"

"Doctor, if it is a tumor and not cancerous, I want it removed. I am tired of hurting," I replied.

"Okay, and this is what we will do. Gabriel, how do you feel about the decision she's made?"

"I feel good. She's making the best decision for her, and what she feels, I feel," Gabriel said.

"Okay then, we will move forward with setting up a schedule for the operation."

"That would be wonderful," Gabriel agreed.

"I will make a few calls and get back to you as soon as possible with a date."

My surgery day came, and we were off to the hospital. The nurse got me prepped while Gabriel stood off in the corner watching. Tears were rolling down his face, dropping onto his chest, as if he could transcend all those tears from his chest into mine, hoping they would heal me through his love.

They began to roll me out of the prep area to the surgical department, with Gabriel walking beside my bed, holding my hand. We made it to the corridor where he could go no further, and he said to me, "Passion, sweetheart, I love you. I love you with all my heart. I know you're coming back, and I am going to wait right here. I am going to be by your side when you open your eyes and see me."

"I love you, Gabriel."

"I love you too, Passion. I will see you when you get back to recovery."

The surgery took about three hours; it seemed like it was forever.

"Finally, the doctor came out to discuss the surgery with Gabriel. "Gabriel, the surgery went well. We were able to remove the whole tumor. We did send some off to the lab, and hopefully, we will hear something from pathology to let us know if it was cancerous. But I do not believe it is, and we're going to remain optimistic."

"Oh, that is such great news, just knowing that you were able to remove the tumor. She's a very strong lady, so do not worry right now. We will just let her make it back to recovery, and once she's out of there, you will be able to see her. She will not be awake because she'll still be under sedation. Once it wears off, she'll be back to herself again. It was a big surgery, so do not expect her to have a conversation with you today. We just want her to rest."

"Okay, doctor, I understand. I just want to see her. I just need to see for myself, hold her hand, kiss her, and tell her I am here.

The doctor told me to go home, get some rest, and come back the next day, but I just could not leave her—not my wife. How could I leave her? I am going to stay in this hospital all night until she wakes up. I want to be the one she sees when she opens her eyes.

HEALING WITH A POSITIVE MIND

*I*t's 1:00 in the morning, and I am sitting here waiting for Passion to wake up so that she can see my face. I wonder if she can sense that I am here, just too weak to say something. Wait a minute, she's moving her arm. I will go over to her bed.

"Passion, it's me, it's Gabriel," I say as I grab her hand, and she squeezes mine. Now I know she knows I am here.

"Oh, Passion, I am so happy everything went fine. The doctor said you are good. They were able to remove the whole tumor, so you do not have to worry. Just rest and get well. I am not going to leave you; I am just going to sit right here in the corner in the recliner until you fully wake up."

Finally, Passion has fully awoken. I can see she is looking around the room to see if she is alone. Her eyes locked onto mine.

"Gabriel, you are here," she says.

"Yes, Passion, I am here. I told you I was not going to leave you."

"Oh, this makes me feel so good. Passion, how are you feeling right now?" Gabriel asks.

"Well, it's hard to say right now. I haven't been able to move, I guess, since they brought me to my room," she continues.

"That is true, Passion, but I know you, sweetheart. Your body is strong and resilient, and you will get better as time goes on. Recovery is a process that will take time. You are so much stronger than the scars left behind, and mentally, I believe you will heal, and we will be able to put this behind us. Just believe and trust in God, and we will get through it all," I reassure her.

"Gabriel, I feel like I have to go to the bathroom."

"Okay, I will get the nurse."

"No, Gabriel, I want to go to the bathroom on my own."

"Passion, you cannot do that. They're not going to let you get up today to go to the bathroom. They have a catheter in you, so you do not move as much, so that is probably what you are feeling."

"A catheter? What is that?"

"It's a tube that they have inserted in you to release urine from your body. The doctor said they will only have it in you for a day, and they will try to get you up and move to see how you do. If you do well, they will remove it. But for now, just work with it, okay? For both of us."

"Okay, Gabriel, I will do my best."

The nurse comes in and asks Passion how she is feeling.

"I really do not know. I thought I had to go to the bathroom, but then Gabriel told me that I did not need to go because I had something inserted in me."

"That is right, Passion. We put the catheter in you so you wouldn't have to move on the first day after surgery. Will they have to keep it in long?"

"Well, Passion, we'll just take it one day at a time. In the meantime, I am going to get in contact with the doctor and let him know that you are awake. We will see what our next move is going to be."

"Okay, that'll be great. Is he going to come in and check on me?"

The nurse asked, "Gabriel, do you have any questions you want to ask me?"

"No, nurse. I do not have any questions right now. I just want to ask the doctor how long he thinks Passion will be in the hospital after this surgery."

"Okay, that is understandable. You have answered a lot of questions already, which is great."

Later that evening, the doctor comes in and asks, "Passion, how do you feel?"

"I feel okay. Did Gabriel tell you how everything went?"

"Yes, he did tell me that you were able to remove the full tumor."

"Yes, we were. Everything was intact, and that was the positive side of the surgery. We were hoping it would happen that way. You initially gave us a little scare, but everything worked out well. Right now, I do not want you to dwell on when you are going home. Just get well enough so that when you do leave, you can stand up and walk to the bathroom on your own. I am looking at maybe two days. If you are strong enough, there is a strong possibility I will release you to go home on one condition."

"What condition would that be, doctor?"

"That you do not go home and overdo it by trying to do housework or cook any meals. Go home, relax, and heal. Gabriel will be there to help you. If you feel that you need a nurse's assistance, we can assign one to come and check on you to help Gabriel if he feels the task may be a little bit too much for him."

Gabriel replied, "I am not going to need any service like that."

"Okay, but if you feel overwhelmed, just call us. In the meantime, she can go back on a full diet in the hospital. There are no restrictions on what she can eat."

"You see, Passion, I told you everything is working its way out, and we're going to be back home in a couple of days so I can take care of you, my beautiful wife. You have a beautiful spirit about you, whether you see it or believe it. I know I see it. The spirit you have is stronger than anything that happens to it. Just look at it as one day stronger than the day before."

"It's been about three days now, and I want to go home, Gabriel."

"I know, Passion. The doctor will be in soon, and we will see what he says and take it from there."

"Okay, but I hope he lets me go home. I really miss my bed."

"Passion, I hear the doctor's out in the hallway. I think they're making their morning rounds. Let us see if he's one of them."

There was a knock at the door, and the nurse and doctor came in to see how I was doing. To my amazement, he asked me if I was ready to go home. I was so excited.

"Yes, doctor, I am ready to go home. I've waited for this day."

"Okay, everything seems to be going well, and your tests came back really good. I do not see any reason why you cannot go home. Just give me a few minutes to get your discharge paperwork together and the medication you will need to take at home in case you have pain."

"Oh, that is just wonderful news. I am so happy."

"Okay now, Passion, I do not want you to go home and overdo it and end up back in the emergency room."

"I promise, doctor, I will not do any of that. I will listen to you so that I can get better. Thank you."

"Gabriel, is there anything else that you feel you may need for her?"

"I do not believe there is anything I need at this moment, doctor."

"Okay then, once I finish up the paperwork, we will have a nurse bring a wheelchair to take her down to the car. Gabriel, I will need you to bring the car up to the loading area so she can get in."

"I will."

Fifteen minutes later, the nurse came into my room with my discharge papers.

"Yay, Gabriel, I am going home."

"Yes, Passion, you are going home, sweetheart. Let me help you get dressed. I did bring you a fresh set of clothes to put on."

"Okay, good."

Finally, I got my clothes on. I am all set and ready to go. I have my discharge paperwork, I am waiting for the nurse to come in with a wheelchair, and I am on my way home. Gabriel went ahead and brought the car to the loading area, and we got into the car and headed back home so I could start my healing process.

"Gabriel?"

"Yes, Passion."

"I love you so much, and I know I put you through a lot by not telling you a long time ago about what I was going through and how I was suffering. Maybe it's because I was afraid something was wrong, and I did not want to believe it. But it got to the point where it became unbearable for me."

"Come on, Passion, we're not going to look back at all of that. We're just going to live in the moment, knowing that everything is taken care of now. We're just going to heal, and that is what we're going to focus on—not thinking about the past."

"Okay, Gabriel."

"Now, I do have to ask you one thing."

"What is that, Passion?"

"Since the doctor says I am on a regular diet, can we do that one thing before we leave for the house?"

"What might that be, Passion?"

"I want my ice cream cone."

"There you go, you can never forget about the ice cream cone."

"No, I guess not, Gabriel. No matter how old I get, it's something that has always been a part of me. You do the same thing, too, because when I get mine, you get your favorite rainbow ice cream."

"No, you got it backward, Passion. You are the one that likes the rainbow."

"No, I do not believe so, Gabriel. You always said that each color had a different flavor."

"Yes, I did say that."

"Well, anyway, if we're going to stop and get ice cream, that is another stop I would like to make before we get to the house. But we have to make sure we eat our ice cream first.

"Oh, there is the place I want to go."

"Where, Gabriel?"

"Do you see over there? Right there, on the corner."

"Yes, Passion, I see that. It's a flower shop. But I have so many already from the hospital."

"That is okay. How many times have I told you a woman can never have too many flowers? And these are your coming home flowers."

"Okay, Gabriel, if you insist."

Gabriel went into the flower shop, but he did not bring me flowers this time. It was a plant. He explained to me why he had chosen to get a plant this time. I could not believe what was coming out of his mouth and the words he used to explain it. It was so touching and so real.

"Passion, when I was a little boy, I would watch my mother plant seeds, not knowing what they were. As I grew older, I came to realize that these seeds were not flower seeds for the garden—they were special herbs she would plant. My mother would cook with those herbs, many of which had healing properties. We did not get sick often growing up. My mother always knew what to give us to combat most ailments."

"You always liked spending time in your garden. I thought this would be something to start with for both of us: the first step to self-healing through the foods we cook. You know it's never too late to start something new, something that is going to help us overall."

"Gabriel, that sounds genuinely nice. But I would like to get some literature to read. I never considered doing anything like this until you mentioned it, but it makes sense. You know I have such a hard time taking all those chemical medications—they really mess with my stomach. I believe if we start making more of our food on a natural basis, it would be better for both of us. We are going to stop eating a lot of processed meats, which have a lot of sodium, and start eating smartly."

"I know it won't be easy, but with our age, it's something to consider. I am going to look online and read up on some of the herbs that my mother used to plant because there are so many—it would be a great start for us. I know it seems like I am more excited than you are to get started but given what has happened to you and having that tumor removed from your body, I believe this would be the best time to start something like this. Even though I know it will take some time for these herbs to grow, in the meantime, we can purchase these herbs at the market."

"Passion, I believe you will feel a difference in your body over time. We cannot just stop taking all your meds right now because you are going to need guidance from the doctor as we transition to other alternatives. It will help us as we move forward to live a better and healthier life."

"Passion, I was so worried about you. I am so glad the doctors found that tumor. If you had never said anything to me, you would have continued to suffer in silence to the point where the doctors would not have been able to do anything for you. We are not going to dwell on it. That part is over; what matters now is that the tumor is out of your body."

"Gabriel, did they really get it all?"

"Yes, Passion, you just need to heal. Promise me that the next time your pain becomes unbearable, you'll let me know."

"Yes, Gabriel, I will let you know. We must focus on your healing now."

"It's getting late, and I want to get dinner started. Would you like something to drink while I prepare it?"

"Yes, can I have a glass of water?"

"Sure, sweetheart, I will be right back. Here you go."

"Thanks, Gabriel."

"No problem. Passion, I wasn't planning on a big meal. Just something light. Is that okay?"

"Yes," Passion replies. "You know, Gabriel, a nice chef salad sounds good."

"If that's what you want, we'll both have it. We have everything for it."

"Wow, Gabriel, this salad is good. Thank you."

"I'm glad you're enjoying it. We finally finished dinner, and I took my medicine. It's time for bed." Gabriel and I made it upstairs. We got our showers, as usual, and went to bed. We both fell asleep after a long day, only to be woken up by the chirping sounds of birds on the windowsill.

"Passion, did you sleep well?"

"Yes, I did. The pain medication really helps."

"That's good. How do you feel about going downstairs and having breakfast?"

"I'm not hungry, but I would love a cup of coffee and some orange juice."

"Okay, let me help you get your housecoat on and make it down to the kitchen."

We finished our coffee and headed back upstairs. Suddenly, I had a sharp pain in my chest as we made it to the top of the staircase. Gabriel hurried to get me back in bed.

"Passion, what was that all about?"

"I'm not sure, but it reminds me of the old pain I had before."

"I don't like the sound of that. I am calling the doctor now."

I'll explain to the receptionist what just happened. She asked if I could bring Passion now. There's an opening for 11 a.m., and I told her we would make it.

"Passion, let me help you get dressed. We're not going to sit on this. Too many things have been going on in your body. We're not taking any chances."

"Okay," Passion replies.

We made it to the doctor's office, and they immediately took us in. Finally, the doctor came in and removed the gauze from Passion's surgical site. Shocked by what he saw, he called radiology for a CT scan. They took her in ahead of everyone else. With her surgery being three weeks old, she should be better than what is showing. The CT was finished, and we headed back to the doctor's office. The results made it back to him before we got there.

Once again, the doctor asked if Passion could wait outside for a minute.

"Doctor, what is it?" Gabriel asked.

"This is not good at all."

"What do you mean it's not good?"

"When the large tumor was removed, small ones started growing in her at an alarming rate. Gabriel, it looks like cancer. We need to do a biopsy today. Can she stay overnight?"

"Of course, she can. Bring her back in so I can explain what's going on and why she is not healing."

"Okay, I will bring her in."

The doctor asked Passion to have a seat. He went on to explain what was going on in her body. Passion collapsed on the floor. Gabriel, the doctor, and the nurse helped pick Passion up off the floor and called EMS. Gabriel was in a panic. The EMS arrived and took Passion to the hospital. Her oxygen had dropped, and her bloodwork was off the charts. They were finally able to stabilize her, but she was in a deep level of pain. Gabriel mustered up the strength to call Paul and Jenny to come to the hospital. They dropped what they were doing and made it there.

"Gabriel, what's going on with Passion?"

Gabriel began to cry.

"Okay now," Paul replies. "This doesn't look good. Tell me, please, what is going on with Passion?"

"Paul, they think it's cancer. We were at home. We made it to the top of the staircase, and Passion nearly passed out with pain traveling through her back, where the rib bone had broken off. They had removed a large tumor that caused it. I guess she's still having something else going on associated with it. I'm not sure. They have already done a CT scan on her. They already wanted her to stay overnight in the hospital for a biopsy. I think they are doing it now."

The hospital doctor came out and told me they would be keeping her until her biopsy results came back. Jenny asked the doctor, "Can anyone stay overnight with her?"

"Yes, you are welcome to stay with her."

Passion finally woke up and saw Gabriel, Paul, and Jenny in the room with her. They did not leave her side that night.

It had been three days, and Passion's biopsy results had come back. Gabriel had just gone to get something to drink. The doctor came back after Gabriel returned, and he had a distant look on his face.

"Gabriel, yes, Passion's biopsy came back. Passion has cancer throughout her chest cavity and organs."

"You can treat this, right?"

"I'm sorry, Gabriel. She is in stage four. Treatment will not help her. The only thing we can do is make her comfortable and try to control her pain."

"Well, if that's all you can do, let me take my wife home with me."

"Are you sure that's what you want to do?"

"Yes."

"I will prepare discharge papers for her and a prescription for pain. She will go into Hospice care, so she will have a nurse assist her so you won't become overwhelmed. She will be transported back home in an ambulance because she will need oxygen. They will hook everything up for her. I am so sorry, Gabriel."

I rushed home to be there when she arrived. Everyone on our street couldn't believe what they were seeing. Not Passion. Paul and Jenny just fell apart. They were just at the hospital. They got Passion in the house and set it up in our bedroom. I will never let her sleep alone. She looked over at me and asked if she could have a cup of coffee.

"Yes, sweetheart, I will get one for you. Anything else?"

"Maybe some orange juice."

I hurried to get what she wanted. I even made myself a cup of coffee.

"Gabriel, this is a good cup of coffee. Thank you."

"Sip it slowly."

"I will."

The nurse from the Hospice came to sit with Passion if I needed to run and get a few things. I said I was okay.

It was getting late, and Passion did not want anything to eat. Tomorrow is our anniversary. I had already gotten her flowers to give her when she woke up in the morning. But right now, I just wanted to climb in bed.

"Gabriel."

"Yes, Passion."

"Can I sleep in your arms tonight?"

"Yes, sweetheart. Let's just hold onto each other."

"Okay."

"Gabriel."

"Yes, Passion."

"I love you so much."

"I love you too."

"Always?"

"Yes, always, till death do us part."

The morning came, listening to the birds chirping on the windowsill.

"Passion, do you hear the birds? Passion, do you hear me?"

Gabriel pulled his arm from around her neck. Eyes wide open, not breathing.

"No, Passion, no. Passion, do not leave me. Please, God, don't take her. Not today. It is our anniversary. She did not get to see her flowers… Oh, my Passion."

The Hospice nurse ran upstairs to console Gabriel. She called the doctor to let them know that Passion had passed. They would be sending a hearse to get her. When it arrived, everyone on the street ran out of their homes, screaming and crying. The poor little children knew what had happened. They began to weep for the mother of the street, who had been there for them and made them laugh. People from all over the neighborhood started showing up, trying to console Gabriel. He had cried so much. Paul and Jenny would not let him be alone. All Gabriel kept saying was…

IT WAS OUR ANNIVERSARY

THE RECIPIENT OF A DONOR'S HEART

Rage simmers beneath my skin like an untamed fire I can't control. I lash out at people who don't deserve it, snapping at friends, pushing away neighbors, punishing the world for a loss it couldn't prevent. But the truth is, my heart is hollow. Our bed is cold where she once lay. The house is quieter without her laughter. No warm hug in the morning, no whispers of 'I love you' before sleep, just silence. Her voice remains in my mind, soft yet insistent, as if she's still here, whispering to me, saying, "Don't let grief swallow your love. You're still here. Live. Love. Cherish what we had, but don't let it chain you to sorrow."

I close my eyes, aching for the warmth of her touch, the way she'd brush her fingers through my hair when I felt troubled. But when I open my eyes, it's just me—just an echo of what used to be. "Do not become this bitter person since I left." I cannot call out your name without a teardrop falling down my face. Passion, I know your journey was not easy in those last days, but when I think about how much you gave to this earth, I know God is taking good care of you—no pain, no more sadness, no sorrow. I am just left with loneliness, a loneliness that is so hard to endure. So, I just go down to my knees and pray at bedtime, asking God for serenity to accept what I cannot change.

I have allowed myself to turn into this bitter person, seeing all our neighbors hold hands and go about their daily chores. But I have no one to hold hands with, so I lash out at everyone, unaware of how it affects them. If anyone had ever told me to be prepared for the day that one of us would be no more, I would have just looked and said, "God would not split us up." But I know this was wishful thinking. I am just this lonely person trying to move forward.

I sit at the breakfast table, my coffee growing cold between my fingers. The morning sun is bright—too bright for a day like this. Outside the window, a family of squirrels scurries along the fence, their tiny paws gripping the bark. I should feel something watching them, maybe amusement or curiosity. Instead, there's just numbness. Even nature carries on without her. My eyes drift to the garden, to the flowers she loved. They sway gently in the breeze, but she isn't there to tend to them anymore. I opened the window to pass a few that I had collected. They ran back to the trees. But from a distance, I can see all the little birds carrying on their daily lives and seeing them is such a pleasant feeling. I glanced down at your garden, where all the beautiful flowers stood, where you should be standing. But you're not there to look up to me anymore.

I remember when we said our vows, especially the part where we promised we would never leave each other." Where one goes, the other one would follow. How could I have imagined you would be the one to leave me? Neither one of us fully understood the depth of that state-ment at the time. God created our hearts, which are shaped the same way on both sides. Somehow, it became divided into two halves. I know death brings a physical departure—a permanent loss. What was once tangible becomes intangible. The spirit lingers on. It's the mental journey I must go through and the most challenging part to overcome.

But deep down inside, my side of the heart is burning within and longing for just one more touch.

Someone knocked at the door. I opened it to see who it was. To my surprise, it was the neighbors on our street: Paul and Jenny, Tom and Casey, and George and Carla. All of them were here to support me.

"Gabriel, is it OK if we come in to talk with you? I know this is a difficult time for you, as it is for all of us. None of us blame you for the harsh words you said. It's expected when you lose someone you love so dearly. It is very painful, and no matter what, we will be by your side."

As the tears began to run down my face, I could not help but grab Paul. He began to cry as well. "Just hold on, Gabriel, and let it all out. We did not want it to come over too soon. You need enough time to absorb what has transpired in your life. We, too, were lost for words."

"Paul, where do I begin? How do I start over?"

"Gabriel" just don't dwell on that right now. Let's take one day at a time. We all brought a dish to help ensure you have something to eat." "I do not believe I can eat anything at this moment, Paul, at least not right this moment."

"Tom, George, thank you so much for coming by. This means so much to me. Seeing you, Carla, especially you, Jenny? You all were the closest to my wife and kids."

"Yes, we were, Gabriel."

"I am so messed up right now; I am sorry. Come on in, have a seat. I am just so wrapped up in my own emotions right now I forgot to tell you to come into the house."

"Gabriel, you just sit down and let us ladies take care of everything right now, and you gentlemen, just sit down and talk with one another. We will get some coffee going and just sit down and talk about those good old times. Times that made us laugh and filled our hearts with joy."

Passion touched everyone's heart she encountered. She had a special aura about her. You knew that her heart was pure and genuine. We all are not going to sit here and talk about the death of Passion; we're going to talk about the good old times.

"Gabriel?"

"Yes, Paul?"

"Do you remember when I lost my first wife? I felt like I was all alone. You were the first one on the street to come to my home to express your condolences. You grabbed onto me and told me it would be alright. So, I do understand your hurt and the pain you are going through. George, you have not said much since you came in and sat down."

"I know, Gabriel. I guess I am still in shock, trying to grasp the gravity of what has transpired and its impact on all of us. I am just lost for words."

"It is OK, George. I've been spending a lot of my time upstairs blaming everybody, being short with my words, not realizing that they were going through the same kind of hurt in a different kind of way. She was my wife, my partner for life. How do you wake up in the morning now, knowing that when you turn over in the bed, she is not there anymore?"

Tom stands abruptly, his chair scraping against the floor. Without a word, he walks out of the room. We hear the door click shut, then—soft at first, barely audible—a muffled sob.

Cassie glances at me, worry etched into her features, then rises and heads toward the bathroom. She knocks gently. "Tom?" No answer. She pushes the door open, and there he is, sitting on the cold tile floor, head in his hands.

"Tom?" she whispers, kneeling beside him.

He lifts his head, and I see the pain in his eyes, raw and unfiltered. His lips tremble. "She was like my sister," he choked out. "She always told me when I was being an idiot, always kept me in line. I don't know how to live in a world where she's not here."

Cassie wipes his tears, whispering words of comfort. I step forward, heart heavy, and kneel beside them. "You're not alone, Tom," I say. "We all lost her."

She knocks at the door and calls out Tom's name. He does not answer. She opens the door, and Tom is sitting on the bathroom floor with a solemn stare in his eyes. "Tom, are you OK?" she asks. Suddenly, a waterfall of tears begins to run down his face.

Cassie helped wipe the tears from Tom's eyes. Gabriel and George came running into the bathroom to help get Tom back into the living room. Tom kept repeating, "Gabriel, I am so sorry. Passion is gone. She was like the big sister I never had. She was always getting on with me about the little things, correcting me when I was wrong, as a sister would do. So, I lost a big part of me as well."

"You know, it is funny how some of us grew up on this same street. Who knew that later in life, some of us would end up living so close to each other," Tom reflects. "I remember when Cassie and I had our first baby, a little girl. We asked if you and Passion would be godparents to our daughter, and you two accepted it. The christening was so beautiful."

"It was, Tom. But she was more than just that to me. She was my big sister. I am going to miss her dearly. I didn't mean to fall apart like that. I guess it was something I had to let out. I am sorry if I scared any of you," Tom says.

"Do not worry about it," Gabriel responds. "I remember when Passion would yell down the street, just three doors down, and say, 'Carla,

Carla, I see you planting new flowers,' and she would reply, 'Yes, I am,' and of course, Passion had to walk down to see what kind of flowers. When I look back on our lives and having Passion around, it always gives me a sense of feeling humbled and blessed to have such a beautiful person around. Someone you can truly call a friend. Someone who was always attentive to other people's needs. Even though we may have lost her physical form, I want to remember all those good memories that resonate in our hearts."

"You know, she had this way of talking to you, and her voice was like her soul in every word she spoke. Her strength was in how she stood up, never bending over. She was a strong woman. Gabriel, she was strong in every form of a woman, wife, mother, and grandmother. She was more than that. To sum it all up in a word, there isn't one to be found," Carla adds.

"Gabriel, it is getting late, and we are going to get ready to leave so you can rest up a little bit. I know you mentioned that your son and daughter will be here tomorrow, so I am sure you have some things to get together for their arrival," Paul says.

"Oh yes, you're right. I will be glad to see them. You know, they are such a pure image of their mother. I know when I see them, I am going to see a part of her in them. Perhaps it will ease it up a little bit for me just to have them close at this time."

The morning has come. I get up, take a shower, and stop for a moment. I keep telling myself she's no longer coming in with me, but I know I must have the strength to continue. I have to hold myself together for the kids. I continue my shower, dry off, get dressed, and make it downstairs to make myself a cup of coffee. Just as I begin to sit down at the table, there's a knock at the door. It is my daughter, Saida. She falls into my arms and begins to cry uncontrollably.

"Daddy, is Mamma gone?" she keeps repeating. "Daddy, is Mama really gone? This cannot be happening to my world. I need my Mama."

"I know, baby, we all do. But it was her time. You know this is the hardest trip I have ever had to take, Daddy. I had to find a way to control my composure so I would not be crying throughout the flight. Everybody felt something was going on with me, but they did not know what it was. The flight attendants kept asking, 'Ma'am, is there anything we can get you?' I kept saying, 'No, there's nothing,' the more I cried, the more they realized I was crying for something sad."

"I stopped crying for a moment and told them that my Mama died, and I was going home for her funeral. The flight attendants began to cry with me. One held onto my hand and said, 'You know, during this flight, focus on the good times to get you through this flight. Do not dwell on her death. Focus on the good times you had with her and laugh. Laugh through all of those tears. Better days are sure to come. You are going to be alright.'" Finally, my flight made it in. I hurried to pick up my luggage and my rental car. Driving through the traffic to get to Daddy. It felt like it took forever. But I made it to the house, tears running down my face. He was waiting for me outside to pull up. I got out of the car. Daddy just grabbed me and just kept saying to me. It is going to be alright. Look at me. You hear what I said? Yes, daddy.

"Daddy, do you mind if I go upstairs and lay on Mom's side of the bed?" Saida asks.

"Sure, baby, go right ahead. Lay down as long as you want. I need this.

Two hours have passed, and I hear another knock at the door. I go to see who it is, and it is Jabril and his family. I looked into his face, and there was a look of deep sadness. He asks me, "Is it true? Is it true that Mom is gone?"

"Yes, son, she is gone."

As he enters the house, he starts looking around the living room. Tears began to fall down his face. He turns around, looks at me, and, without a word, drops to his knees in front of the couch where his mother always sits. He keeps screaming, "Mom, Mom, I need you. How could this be? Why did God take you away from me?"

I ran over to my son and kneeled beside him. His wife, Fatima, and their kids began to cry due to his outpouring of tears. She took the kids into the kitchen. I stayed kneeling beside my son. I heard Sima coming down the stairs. She hurried over and ran to both of us. We all embraced, wiping away each other's tears.

Finally, we regain our composure and begin to laugh. Saida tells Jabril, "I never knew you could cry like that."

"Do not tease me. That little boy is still there, and every now and then, he comes out. But today, I felt like a little boy, Momma's little boy. It is OK, Jabril."

"Sima, I bet you cried like a baby, too, am I right?"

"Yes, I did. We know girls are very emotional. Well, I am not going to deny it. Yes, I cried in Daddy's arms."

"Look at you two, carrying on as you always have from little kids to now. What amazes me is that you two are so supportive of each other, never hurting each other's feelings. I see your mother in both of you. It eases my pain to see you two."

"Oh, Saida, Jabril brought his wife Fatima and kids with him. They are in the kitchen."

"That is wonderful. John and my kids will not be here until tomorrow. I just wanted to hurry up and get here."

"OK, now, with all my visits yesterday and today, I think we have built a river of tears and sadness. Now, we must focus on strength and talk about happier times. Remember what your mom left behind: her love for life, her love of family, and the people she touched."

"You are right, Dad," Saida and Jabril reply.

It is getting late. With so much company this evening, it has really drained me. You know where everything is. Just make yourselves home as always. I really need to lay down. We can continue planning the next move after we plan your mom's service, "Celebration of Life."

I understand, Daddy, Saida replies.

The morning comes, and Saima and Fatima have cooked breakfast. Jabril knocked at my bedroom door. Dad, come on down. Breakfast is ready. Okay, let me get up and brush my teeth. Okay, let me get up, brush my teeth, and wash my face. I will be right down.

I made it downstairs. Wow, that smells so good. Come on, Daddy. Daddy, sit next to me. Jabril is getting you a cup of coffee. Good morning, everyone. It feels so good to see you all this morning. Family. This means so much to me right now.

After everyone had eaten, the kitchen was cleaned up. We all took showers and dressed. We must head off to the funeral home to make plans for Passion.

"Daddy, do you think it is possible that we could pick out a bright color for Momma's casket, not anything dark?"

"Sure, Saida, we can pick whatever you want. Jabril, what do you think about that?"

"It is OK; let Saida pick everything for Mom," Jabril replied.

"Do you want a private service, or do you want something on a larger scale? You must remember your mother had many friends, and a lot of people loved her, so we have to find somewhere that can accommodate a lot of people."

"I think the chapel will be big enough."

"OK, then we will plan to have it in the chapel because they do hold up to 500 people. If it exceeds that amount, I am sure there will be people outside, but we can ask to set up speakers outside the chapel with a large screen so those who cannot make it inside can see everything that is going on inside."

"Oh, Daddy, that would be wonderful."

We finally made it to the funeral home and explained to the Director what we would like to have for our mother's service. The funeral home was a tranquil, welcoming space with soft lighting and soothing music designed to provide comfort during difficult times. We described the bright, uplifting colors we wanted for the casket, the flower arrangements, and the overall atmosphere that would celebrate her life.

The Funeral Director, a kind and compassionate man with a gentle demeanor, listened carefully to all our requests. He was detailed, noting every detail to ensure that our wishes were honored.

"Gabriel," the Funeral Director said, his voice sincere and empathetic. "Let me say, first of all, I am so sorry for your loss. We will do the best we can to make her homecoming as beautiful as the person you described to us. Please let us know if you would like to have anything else."

THE CELEBRATION OF PASSION'S LIFE

"There comes a time in our lives when we must say goodbye to those we love. Even through sad times, we must find the strength to smile through laughter and tears. Passion was a special kind of person. Not just my wife, she was first someone's daughter, then my wife, a mother, a grandmother, and a friend to many."

"Today, I ask all of you to celebrate her life and not dwell on her death. During all my pain, I found so much joy in her life and the lives she touched. As I look out at all of you in the congregation, I realize how many people she truly impacted. I thank you more than you will ever know. Many of you knew her for her soft-spoken words and her gentle heart."

"God blessed us with two beautiful children, Jabril and Saida. Together, they gave us five wonderful grandchildren. Passion's world lit up whenever she saw them. They brought her so much joy."

"I will not stand up here and go on and on about how beautiful Passion was and how she touched every one of you. She was my every morning, day, and night. One thing I will say is that I am glad you all got to know her and gave her flowers while she was alive because she truly loved flowers. Many of you want to get up here and speak on her behalf. We have the time to allow as many of you as you want to express her impact on your lives. But please make it brief."

"Hold on a moment, is that Liam?

"Yes, it is me."

"Can I say something, Mr. Gabriel? Can I come up there?"

"Yes, Liam, come on up here. Is there something you would like to say?"

"Yes, I want to talk about Mrs. Passion. She was very nice to us and all the kids around the neighborhood. Sometimes, when the ice cream truck came around, she would see all the kids running to catch it, and some of us didn't have money for ice cream. She would walk up to see who did not have money, and, of course, many of us did not. She would always buy our ice cream for us. It is like she always knew. Mrs. Passion loved to see us smile and have something cold to eat on hot days. It made us feel good."

"Sometimes, we would see her out planting in her garden, and she would always yell at us, 'You little kids doing good?' We would reply, 'We are doing OK,' and then she would ask us about our school day. We would say, 'It was good, Mrs. Passion.' She cared about what we were doing, and it made us feel good. I am going to miss her. Mrs. Passion was like the mother of the neighborhood to all of us. That is all I have to say, Mr. Gabriel. I love you, Mrs. Passion. I am going to miss you."

Liam began to walk back to his seat. Suddenly, he stopped right in front of the coffin. With flowers in his hand, Liam placed them next to her picture and spoke. "These are for you, Mrs. Passion. I picked them from your garden. I hope it's okay." Liam made a small gesture by kissing her picture.

Finally, Liam made it back to his seat. Tears fell from everyone's faces, moved by the words he spoke so gently about Passion. You could tell this kid had a heart for someone who was truly kind to him. Gabriel continued to say that Liam's words were touching.

After all the children saw how Liam went up to the podium to talk about Miss Passion, they stood up and began walking up to her casket, each wanting to speak about her. Finally, Misty reached the microphone and expressed her deep sorrow. She looked at Mr. Gabriel and all the congregation's people, not knowing what to say because there was so much to say about Miss Passion as she began to speak. She said, "Miss Passion was like the mother in the neighborhood, just like Liam said. She always made us laugh, and just like how she brought us ice cream, she always kept candy by her front door. Each one of us kids, when we wanted something sweet to eat, it was always there for us. We did not take a whole lot; we just took a couple of pieces of candy so all the other kids could get some, too. Miss Passion always knew when the candy was running low because she always kept it full for us. There were times when she would look out the window and see us kids taking candy, and she would smile at us and say, 'It's OK, baby. Get what you want.' That's all I want to say about Miss Passion."

Misty also had a flower to place in the basket by Passion's picture as she walked down from the podium. She walked over to it and placed it there next to Liam's flower.

It was Cheryl's turn to come up, tears rolling down her face, and carrying a flower in her hand in honor of Miss Passion. She began to speak into the microphone, looking out into the audience with a broken voice. She said, "Roses are red, violets are blue. I am going to miss you too." The people began to cry, shocked by the words coming out of this child's mouth. As she began to leave, she carried her flower over to Miss Passion's picture and walked past her casket, gazing at it as if she were saying, "My neighborhood mom is gone." Little Cheryl's mother had to get her because Cheryl could not find enough strength to walk back to where she was seated.

As Cheryl's mother grabbed her, Cheryl said, "Mommy, please do not take me away from her. Let me stay with her for a little while longer." Cheryl's mother replied, "Sure, but we have to make it back to our seats so the other children can speak."

"I know, Mommy, but I just do not want to leave her right now. Please, Mommy, just let me sit by her, please." One of the pallbearers grabbed a little chair for Cheryl to sit on right next to Miss Passion's picture. Her tears began to slow as if she could hear Miss Passion telling her it was going to be all right.

Finally, Ava came up. She was praying and asking God to help her heal her heart so she would not be so sad. The adults in the congregation had a big outpouring of tears to the point where people were whispering about how Cheryl had so much passion in her heart for someone who treated her so kindly.

Ava mustered up enough strength to climb the stairs to the podium, but she was assisted to make it there. Being short, Ava stepped up on the stool to reach the microphone and began to tell her story. She shared how, as a little girl, she was considered a special needs child, and no one wanted to play with her. Miss Passion saw that and came over to Ava, telling her to hold her head up and that she had friends; they just had not made it to her yet and to stop crying.

Ava just wanted somebody to play with, someone who looked at her, not her disability, and did not tease her. Miss Passion was right because Ava did get a few friends who played with her and helped her with things she could not do. They were not ashamed of her. Ava finished her speech, holding the flower in her hand. She walked down past Passion's casket and over to her picture, where a basket of flowers sat beside Cheryl and Misty. No one wanted to leave Miss Passion's casket.

All of a sudden, children all over the chapel began to walk down. They all corralled around Miss Passion's picture as if she were reading a storybook to them, as she did in life. It gave the children a sense of comfort, and everything finally calmed down.

Suddenly, a three-year-old little boy named Hunter came walking, crying his little heart out. He remembered Miss Passion, who used to play with him. When he got to her casket, he saw her picture and said, "Mommy, it's Miss Passion." Hunter's mom came down to assist him, but Hunter was not having it; he just kept saying, "No, Mommy, no." With his little flower on his lapel, he took it off and went over to where the other children were, placing it in the basket of flowers. He looked at her picture and said, "I have a flower for you too, Miss Passion."

You could hear the people in the congregation constantly whispering, "Have you seen anything like this before?" The children were so touched and moved by her generosity in life that they had the courage to walk up alone to speak about how she had touched them.

After the children finished, Passion's daughter, Saida, walked up to the podium to talk about her mother and the lives she had touched. Saida went on to say that with the speeches the children gave about their mother, there was not much left to say. But she did say, "She was my mother; she was my kid's grandmother. She was someone I could call morning, noon, and evening, and she always had the time to talk to me no matter what she was doing. She had an ear for listening, not just hearing what you were saying but paying attention to what you were saying. I remember when I was a little girl living on the ranch, my mother and father taught my brother Gabriel and me how to ride a horse. Of course, we would fall off the horse, only to get back up and try again until we could hold ourselves up. I guess what I'm trying to say is that no matter how many times I fell in my life, I was always able to pick myself back up based on my mother's teachings and my atti-tude of not giving up."

"'Beauty and Stallion' were the names of the horses that my brother Jabril and I received when we were fifteen and sixteen years of age. Many years ago, we moved away from the ranch but kept our horses at the stables. About every weekend, we would go and ride them and groom them."

"I do want to say this: I was surprised to see that as we walked into the chapel, to the right of me, I saw the two horses that my mother and father bought for Jabril and me, Beauty and Stallion. I really want to thank the people who took care of them for bringing them because they are also part of our family. For you, Mommy, I am going to miss you so much. I know there will be days when it is going to be hard for me, but I am going to reach down deep inside my heart to find that peace you always talked about. I am going to pick up the pieces and carry them with me throughout my life. As I look up and see the rainbow, I am just going to smile and think about you."

Finally, Saida made it back to her seat. Gabriel said he was happy that he had impacted Passion's life and the lives of other children in the neighborhood. Everyone who spoke in the short time we spoke very fondly of Passion, sharing special moments they will always cherish. Jabril made it to the podium. As he began to talk about his mother's life, he said very softly, "At one time, I was my momma's little boy. That little boy grew to be a young man, taught to be strong and hold his head high. Everyone knows that men cry too, and sometimes the tears are uncontrollable. When you look back on your life and all the good times you had growing up, it is hard to describe because there are not enough hours in a day to talk about my mother and the impact she has had on my life and my family."

"But as I stand before you today, that little boy still resides in me. If I take a lot of breaks in between my words to express the love I have for my mother, please understand that tears show compassion. The tears I shed give thanks to my mother for the person she was. My father and mother were a pure example of what love was all about in marriage. I have learned a lot from them. My mother touched many of you in so many ways, both mentally and physically. I look down on you, Mama, and thank you. I will stand tall and hold my head high because I know you will be looking down at me. I love you, Mom, until we see each other again."

Jabril made it back to his seat, consoled by his sister and his father. Crying uncontrollably, Saida told him, "It's OK, Jabril, we are going to get through this." He rested his head on his sister's shoulder.

Many families and friends had the opportunity to speak, and so many outpourings of love surrounded the whole chapel. There was no room for people to sit. People were standing outside, and there were speakers for everyone to hear the service that was going on over a big screen placed outside.

Gabriel went up to the podium and looked at his two children as they continued to weep. He told them, "Jabril and Saida, we are going to make it through this. We are going to hold on to the memories and cherish them. She left us a large collection of memories to carry on. Cry if you must because, in the end, smiles will be the small things that make a difference in our lives. I want to thank you all for coming to my wife's celebration of life. Let us all leave with fond memories. These memories will sustain us for the rest of our lives. So, as you pass by someone's flower garden, think about Passion; that is how she was to a lot of people: a bouquet of flowers."

The minister made his way to the podium to conduct the eulogy. As he began to speak words of comfort and condolence, somehow, we all found solace in his words. A reality was unfolding before our very eyes. He said, "There cannot be life without death. We have been on this earth for a short length of time. We must do all we can, learn to love, grieve, and let go so that we can move on. I am not going to stand up here and preach a sermon about Passion. You all had your own stories. In many ways, you all have conducted your own eulogy. So, I ask you all to bow your heads in prayer."

"God, in this very moment of overwhelming thoughts and deep emotions, we turn to you to be our refuge and strength. We know that when you call us home one by one, this grief makes us all feel insurmountable. So, we have become saddened with this grief, and even the simplest tasks can feel impossible. We pray, God, we thank you for your immeasurable love. Bless us that we may be honored as we celebrate life and be glorified. And help us get through this suffering of this great loss so that we may find comfort in your arms of love. For our other loved ones for whom the heavens have already opened doors, there is another one standing at the gates. Open your door once again, glorified, and let her see you face to face. We are not here today to mourn Passion's life. We are here to celebrate the life of Passion and all whom she has touched. In your name, we pray. Amen."

"I ask you all to continue to stand as Passion's casket is taken out of the chapel with the family following behind her. The rest will follow behind the family."

Gabriel watched as they loaded Passion into the horse-drawn carriage, tears streaming down his face. He just kept repeating her name, "Passion." Jabril and Saida came over to their dad and said, "It's OK, Dad. We are here for you. We are all here. We have to be strong for Mom." Gabriel replied, "I know it is really hard on you right at this moment. I look around at all the people whose lives she touched. I really did not realize there were so many. Just look at the streets; people are standing and cannot enter the chapel. Have I really married a wonderful person, someone who was touched by so many? Why would God take her away from me? I know I'm speaking selfishly, but at this moment, I am hurting. I am hurting deep inside."

The chauffeur from the limousine summoned us to come on and get in so we could start the procession to the cemetery. It was an hour's ride through all the traffic, with so many people.

We finally made it to the cemetery, and the horses carrying Passion came to a standstill. Finally, they removed her from the carriage.

There was a mist in the air; you could tell that it had been raining earlier. "Saida, Jabril," Gabriel said. "Yes, Dad, what is it?" they replied. "Look over to the left and tell me what you see. I just want to make sure that my eyes are not playing tricks on me, but what do you see?"

"There, there is a rainbow."

"So, do you see it?"

"Yes, Dad, we do."

They turned back around to focus on Mom and the horses that carried her casket. The horses had a stance about them. Suddenly, they lowered their heads as if showing respect for Passion, someone who understood the loss of one's unselfish love. Animals have an instinct to feel lost and compassion.

Gabriel was surprised to see that they had allowed Saida and Jabril's horses, Beauty and Stallion, to come to the cemetery, which is exceedingly rare. Beauty, draped in a colorful rainbow sash, walked gracefully up to the right side of Passion's casket. She stood there, still and serene. Stallion, wearing his sash, the same colorful rainbow colors, followed Beauty and stood on the left side of the casket. They each held a bouquet of flowers in their mouths and gently placed them on top of her casket. Then, they stepped back and knelt, bowed their heads, and lowered them as if in deep respect. Tears began to run from their eyes, and they would not move.

Everyone had a turn to place a flower on top of Passion's casket. When they finished, Gabriel stood up with a bouquet of flowers he had bought for passion on their anniversary. She never got the chance to see the bouquet. Gabriel placed them on her casket, whispering softly. Passion, you passed on our anniversary. I did not make it to the hospital in time to give them to you before you transcended. Happy anniversary, sweetheart. I will always love you.

The cemetery attendants began to lower Passion's casket. Suddenly, the rainbow in the sky grew even larger. The sun shone brightly, making the rainbow's colors sparkle in the sky, filling the world with bright and beautiful shades of flowers that you once planted in your garden.

RELEASING OF THE DOVE

Yesterday, we all celebrated Passion's life and the impact she had on everyone she touched. She lay in a bed of flowers that surrounded her coffin. It was a day I never wanted to see. I know life goes on, and with that, healing follows.

Morning has arrived, and a new day is starting. Finding ways to laugh in the mist of my loneliness. All I really want is to talk to you, Passion, here in our room. I want to thank you for the happiness you've brought into my heart.

There is something I want to finish that we never got the opportunity to do. I want to return to the mountain where we once tried to climb, but we had to stop due to your injury. I want to carve our name on the rock. Starting from our previous point, I will proceed until I achieve that goal.

I know there will be many days when I find myself talking to myself, but it is the only way I know how to cope with the loss. I know I must make this journey alone, but it has a purpose. I will make my flight arrangements to return to Indonesia in the coming days. Have my bags already packed. Loaded in the car. Just in case they have one leaving the next day. I have all my documents. I need to reach the airport in time for a last-minute flight.

I remember you telling me, make sure we have plenty of water before we make that climb. There is one more thing I will bring as well, a first aid kit just in case.

It has been a few days, and I have made it back to the mountains. This time, I brought something incredibly special that I will be carrying with me as I climb to the top of the mountains, something I bought in the city before the tour guide made it to the mountain. There are a lot of things I want to talk to you about. Here I go, starting my climb.

I have been climbing for about 20 minutes now. I need to take a break and sip some water before continuing. I will repeat this until I make it to the top. Wow, three hours have passed, and I have finally made it up here. It is such a beautiful place, Passion.

Oh, I wish you were here to share in this beautiful sight—with all this beautiful land and so many mountains. Passion, when I think about my heartache and the love we shared in our hearts, it was worth it all. Knowing I will always have a collection of memories, a treasure box full of them, I cannot help but feel this emptiness in my soul. I know my grief is not a disorder but an emotional, physical, and spiritual necessity. Passion what I am trying to say that I know it is the consequence of our bond, which we show both physically and openly. I have been beating myself up, asking God why her.

I constantly cry with this endless flow of tears running down my face. Finally, I found the strength to make it here. Sitting atop of this mountain, looking at all the beauty surrounding me. It is a place where I wanted to have some private time to talk to you about things I couldn't say during your celebration of life service. I guess, in a way, it is my way of letting go. Maybe it is my Eulogy to you. While sitting here, I look up above, as if I am looking into heaven. Asking why there is so much pain in losing a loved one. God, you gained an angel that day. In a way, that alone gives me some sort of comfort. Passion, seeing birds flying above me, I brought a white dove with me. I kissed its head and released it over the mountains, a symbol of our love in your honor. I see the beauty, a sight I may never see again.

When I look over our life from the very beginning, how we played as little children, and the first time I saw you, there was this connection. I did not know where it was going to go, but I looked where it took us. The triumphs that we went through to be able to love each other openly. Fighting with my parents, for the woman I chose to love. Made every fight worth it. I stood before my father as a man. Reflecting on my identity as an American and the freedom to choose my path with our parents' blessings, I believe that even with existing boundaries, they can be overcome to allow our love to prevail. We can talk about loving someone and needing them in our lives. But we have no control over what the heart wants or who the heart wants to love. I think about our children, and our precious grandchildren. They are a piece of us you left behind for me to hold on to and to keep your memories alive. I thank God for having them in my life.

Passion, there was a night, I could not sleep. I woke up, went downstairs, and prepared a hot cup of coffee. I even made one for you, not realizing. You are not here anymore. I composed a letter addressed to you. And it reads as follows:

To you, my love:

I am trying so hard to find the strength to triumph. Watching you suffer was a tragedy for me. I prayed so hard that God would just take you out of your pain so you would not suffer anymore. But you know, Passion, I am going to turn this into a triumph. I am going to survive the loss. You see when I lost my mother, you took me by the hand and said to me, "It is ok to cry, sweetheart. Go ahead and put on those sneakers and blue jeans. That little boy is still in you. Shed as many tears as you need. Your mother may not be here anymore. But I am here now to wipe away your tears. Go ahead and rest your head on my shoulder. I will carry you through your pain and sorrow." Losing you, Passion, is so hard, a different kind of loss, to come to terms with. I know you are in a better place than me, a new home, a different dimension where there is no suffering.

I was sitting on the couch where you used to sit all the time. Wishing you were present to provide comfort and advise me to refrain from crying. I started having this intense pain in my chest. I did not know what was happening to me. At that moment, I understood that my heart was experiencing significant distress, to the extent that it felt as though it might fail. I really thank Paul for coming over to check on me because if it had not been for him, I would not have been able to write this letter to you. But who knew the power of love?

I started looking around the room and saw a bottle of champagne at our bar. The kind you loved so much, the one we always opened during our wedding anniversaries. It hurts so much, maybe because you passed on our anniversary. It was devastating to me.

I opened the bottle and poured a glass. I tried so hard to find a reason to celebrate. I just stared at it, watching the bubbles disappear one by one. I closed my eyes for a bit, only to reopen them. The rich and crisp sounds of those bubbles started talking to me. "Gabriel, you are not in the right frame of mind to allow your lips to touch the rim of this glass. It is not an addiction you need when your world falls apart. Don't use me as a replacement for losing your wife. I might spend the rest of your life. Riding on your back. Pull yourself together and live for the memories."

 Finally, I drifted off to sleep and heard someone calling out my name. "Gabriel, it is me, Passion. I am coming to you through your dreams to help bring you comfort and closure. You did not know it, but I came back when you released the dove in my honor and watched the dove fly away. I watched you cry, coming up and going back down the mountain. You are not fully willing to release me, because you still believe I am still here. You are still in your dream state of mind. And I am going to talk to you through your dreams. I want you to travel back to the mountaintop. When you make it there, tell me what you see."

"I made it and saw a dove just sitting there, Passion, what are you trying to tell me."

"I want you to go and sit right next to it. Let your mind flow. You see, Gabriel, I cannot let you continue crying and mourning me. You received a new heart. The first heart you had broken into a million pieces after I passed. When your grief became so unbearable, the heart began to struggle, fighting to the point where it could not handle it anymore. I cannot allow you to grieve so much that you lose your new heart. I am going to keep you in this state of dreaming so that when you wake up, you will feel contentment in your heart. You see, Gabriel, I am sitting here in the palm of God's hand, he is holding me for a while. He allowed me to watch you suffer. I had to come back to you through your dream state of mind and set your pain free so that you will not continue suffering the loss of me."

"Gabriel, I want you to do something for me."

"What is that, Passion?"

"Preserve the heart that you have. Take good care of it so that one day you will be able to love again. The reality of death, sweetheart, is that you will never see me in that form again, but you will remember me through our children, grandchildren, and in your mind, heart, and soul."

"Gabriel."

"Yes, Passion."

"In your dream state, let us have a dance to our favorite song, 'One in a Million.'"

"Oh, Passion, I would love that."

Passion and I danced all night long. We held each other and kissed as if she was still alive, for the last time. The morning was coming, and Passion said to me, "One last time, I love you, Gabriel. Out of nowhere. It felt like Passion touched my heart. Grabbed ahold of my hand, as if she was telling me. She is still here. Is this really a dream? I must go now Gabriel." As the sun began to shine through my window, awakening me with a release of all the pain and sorrow I had felt. I got out of bed and walked over to look out the window. I see that it had been raining during the night. There is a rainbow, I knew then it was you. "Passion."

So now, when rainy days are there, I look around to see if there is a rainbow. I just smile and say, "There goes that bouquet of flowers; isn't she beautiful."

Today is a new day. I feel good in my body, heart, and soul. I have joy and happiness now. I want to just shout to the world and tell everybody that pain does not last long, but with the power of God, all things are possible. The first thing I want to do this morning is get myself together and get out of this house. It is time to start living again. I opened all the cards I'd received from Passion's Celebration of Life downstairs. The one that stood out to me the most was a handwritten card from a little girl. She said, "Mr. Gabriel, when my baby sister died, I was mad at God because he took her from me. She was the only little sister I had. But someone touched me on my shoulder, making me feel good. His voice told me, 'I gave you your sister for a little while, but I need her back.' Mr. Gabriel, that could only be God talking to me. After He finished talking to me, I felt a whole lot better. You're going to get better too, Mr. Gabriel; you just wait and see."

That card had the most impact on me, coming from a child. I know now that I am going to be ok. I grabbed my car keys and closed the door. Paul was watering his plants as I opened the garage door and backed out. I yelled at him, "Paul, have you had breakfast yet?"

"No, Gabriel, why?"

"Come on and go with me. Let's both get out and go enjoy the day."

Paul came over and got in the car.

"Gabriel, what is going on with you? I have not seen you this happy in a long time. What has come over you?"

"Paul, you would not understand."

"Try me."

Gabriel began to tell him about his dream. Paul could not believe what he was hearing. Gabriel, you are carrying on as if Passion is still alive. Suddenly, Paul said, "Gabriel, when Jenny died, she came to me in my dreams as well. I did not tell anyone because I did not want them to think I was delusional."

As time passed, Paul and Gabriel went on with their lives to enjoy what was left behind.

WWGD

ACKNOWLEDGMENTS

I would like to take a moment to express my deepest gratitude to the amazing people who have been pillars of strength throughout my life.

To my husband, your unwavering support, unconditional love, and steadfast partnership are among the greatest blessings of my life. You are my rock, my confidant, my dearest friend, and my constant source of encouragement. Words cannot fully express how grateful I am for your presence in my life. Thank you for always being by my side.

To my beloved mother. Juanita, and my father, Charles E. McGrone. Who are no longer with us. Your gentle and wise words have shaped who I am. You taught me the power of kindness and the importance of extending encouraging words to others. These lessons remain in my heart and guide me on my journey. Thank you to my parents for your enduring love and influence.

My children brought me the greatest joy.

To my son, Damonne, whose presence graced our lives but is no longer with us. His desire to surpass expectations continues to inspire and guide us all. His spirit remains a beacon of strength and determination.

To my daughter, Latieca, you have achieved so much. Yet too much To put in words. Thank you for what you have shown and given over the years.

To my son Michael, you have been my listening ear, always there with unwavering encouragement. Time and again, you remind me, "Mom, there is nothing out there too big for you to challenge." Your words are not just a comfort but a source of strength, pushing me forward when I need it most. I am so proud of the strength and integrity you continue to show.

To my son Jermaine, your courage in life's challenges has been inspiring. Each trial you've encountered has strengthened your character, shaping you into the person you are today.

To my son, Larry Jr, your wisdom and patience are evident in your calm demeanor and positive actions.

To my son, Samuel, stay steady and follow your dreams.

To my brothers, Leonard and his wife Paula, Charles, James, and Stephen and his wife Andrea, you have been the force behind me in creating this book. You reminded me that I was shortchanging the world by not embracing one of my greatest potentials. You encouraged me to transform my dreams of being a screenwriter into becoming an author. You have recognized the hidden talents that reflect my personality, never being surprised by the next level of creativity I might reach. Your belief in me made all the difference. For that, I thank you deeply.

To my baby sister Sarah Garrett, the youngest of us all. From high school to now, you have excelled beyond your years in the educational department. Constantly achieving new heights.

To my other siblings, Kimberly, Tammie, Michelle, Roxanne, Lori, Michael, Rodney, Jamie and Kenyon. Thank you for your highs and lows. Your love and shared laughter have been a source of strength and comfort. Each of you has played a role in me becoming the person I am today. For that, I thank you all.

Lastly, I thank Marilyn, Dot, Marie, and Gary, my beloved sisters and brother, who have long since passed away. Your presence in my life was a gift, and I am forever grateful for the moments we shared. Though you're no longer here, the time you gave me remains in my heart, a treasure I will always cherish.

www.ingramcontent.com/pod-product-compliance
Lightning Source LLC
Chambersburg PA
CBHW070831160726
48004CB00001B/332